READING AND RECALL IN L1 AND L2:
A SOCIOCULTURAL APPROACH

CONTEMPORARY STUDIES IN SECOND LANGUAGE LEARNING
A Monograph Series Dedicated to Studies in Acquisition and Principled Language Instruction

Robert J. Di Pietro, editor

The Catalan Immersion Program: A European Point of View
Jospe Maria Artigal

A Developmental Psycholinguistic Approach to Second Language Teaching
Traute Taeschner

Vygotskian Approaches to Second Language Research
James P. Lantolf and Gabriela Appel, editors

Bilingual and Testing: A Special Case of Bias
Guadalupe Valdes and Richard Figueroa

Elizabeth B. Bernhardt, editor

Listen to the Silences: Mexican American Interaction in the Composition Classroom and Community
Kay Losey

Input Processing and Grammar Instruction in Second Language Acquisition
Bill VanPatten

Words Into Worlds: Learning a Second Language Through Process Drama
Shin-Mei Kao and Cecily O'Neil

Reading and Recall in L1 and L2: A Sociocultural Approach
Regina Roebuck

READING AND RECALL IN L1 AND L2: A SOCIOCULTURAL APPROACH

By Regina Roebuck
University of Louisville

Ablex Publishing Corporation
Stamford, Connecticut
London, England

Printed in the United States of America

Library of Congress Cataloging-in-Publication Data

Roebuck, Regina.
    Reading and recall in L1 and L2 : a sociocultural approach / by Regina Roe-buck.
        p.   cm. — (Contemporary studies in second language learning)
        Includes bibliographical references and index.
        ISBN 1-56750-411-6 (cloth)—ISBN 1-5670-412-4 (pbk.)
        1. Second language acquisition. 2. Discourse analysis - Psychological aspects. 3. Reading comprehension. 4. Recollection
(Psychology).   I. Title.   II. Series.
    P118.2.R59   1998
    401' .93—dc21   98-28085
                                                                        CIP

Ablex Publishing Corporation   Published in the U.K. and Europe by:
100 Prospect Street   JAI Press Ltd.
P.O. Box 811   38 Tavistock Street
Stamford, CT 06904-0811   Covent Garden
                                            London WC2E 7PB
                                            England

For my grandmother, Frances C. Beringer

Contents

Acknowledgments

I would like to express my appreciation to those people without whom this book would not have been possible: I thank Series' Editor Elizabeth Bernhardt for her helpfulness, and especially Jim Lantolf and Gabriela Appel for their guidance and assistance in this project. I give particular thanks to Rick Donato for his thoughtful discussions. Finally, I thank Sarah J. Parrott for her steadfast support and encouragement.

Preface

Reading is a complex process that has been investigated in the second language literature from both reader-driven and text-driven approaches, as well as from frameworks which attempt to unify the two positions. The purpose of this book is to explore text comprehension from a Sociocultural perspective and, in doing so, to discover more about the ways in which readers comprehend and recall native and non-native texts. Specifically, the first and second language literacy of L2 learners of Spanish will be investigated through a Sociocultural analysis of written recall protocols.

The recall task has been used in recent years as a means of assessing text comprehension, both in the L1 and the L2. Researchers have argued that recall protocols, when written in the native language, are an effective way of measuring the comprehension that has occurred at the time of reading. However, research in oral text recall (Appel, 1986, Appel & Lantolf, 1994) has also indicated that the protocols themselves may be evidence of continued comprehension. That is, readers continue to build a comprehension model of the assigned text through talking or writing about it

While many analysis of recall protocols focus on propositional content or an analysis of reader error, Sociocultural Theory provides us with an additional analytic tool: the language of the protocols. This follows from Vygotsky's fundamental insight that thought and language are intrinsically related. Vygotsky argued that speech, in addition to its communicative function, bears a private, self-oriented function, and thus, is used to organize and carry out mental activity. When faced with cognitive difficulties, speakers often externalize their inner order as speech in order to achieve and maintain control of their mental activity in the task at hand (Frawley & Lantolf, 1985). Researchers working within the framework of Sociocultural Theory have found that this overt, organizing speech for self—referred to as private speech or private writing—differs in form from communicative speech in that it is more abbreviated and manifests seemingly aberrant formal properties (e.g. Frawley & Lantolf, 1985; DiCamilla & Lantolf, 1994). Thus, the identification and analysis of privately-oriented writing in the recall protocols collected in this study ought to shed light on the processes involved in comprehension and recall.

An important component of Sociocultural Theory is Activity Theory, which is predicated on the belief that human activity is a complex process, determined by the context, the goals, and sociocultural history of the participants and thus necessarily differs between and even within individuals (A. N. Leontiev, 1981). Along those lines, Coughlin and Duff (1994) have argued that the behavior found in classroom and experimental conditions is neither constant nor controllable because it is an instantiation of activity. They posit a clear distinction between task and activity, and propose that tasks are merely "behavior blueprints", motivated by the researchers' or teachers' agenda and imposed on learners. In comparison, activity is the behavior that is actually produced when tasks are performed (Coughlin & Duff, 1994). Therefore, although the learners in this study were assigned a common set of tasks, we can expect to see diversity in the activity that was realized. The key to discovering this diversity, again, will lie in the language of the protocols.

The study presented in this book investigates text comprehension and recall through a Sociocultural analysis of written recall protocols. Following Vygotsky's insight into the nature of language and cognition, the investigation focuses on the linguistic features of the protocols. Through its constructivist orientation and Sociocultural perspective, this book hopes to contribute to an improved understanding of what it means to read and, particularly, to recall, second language texts in the context of both second language reading research and practice.

The book also hopes to serve as an introduction to Sociocultural Theory and to demonstrate the usefulness of this type of analysis, not only of written recall protocols, but of other forms of learner language. Importantly, the findings presented here ought to contribute to the ever growing body of Sociocultural second language research, particularly to work done in the areas of mediation and private writing and speech.

Finally, the book attempts to illustrate the nature of activity in relation to task, by showing the diverse ways in which learners approached the task of writing a recall protocol. Specifically, it is hoped that the activity-based analysis of task-generated behavior in this book will lead to an awareness of learners as individual agents involved in shaping their activity, based on their own particular goals, motives, and sociocultural history.

This books is organized as follows: The first two chapters present the theoretical framework which will be utilized in the remaining three chapters to explain the learners' behavior in the task of producing a written recall protocol. Chapter 1 presents a brief overview of some of the current perspectives on reading comprehension. Ultimately, a constructivist or meaning-making view of text comprehension and recall will be adopted. Chapter 2 presents some of the relevant features of

Sociocultural Theory, the Vygotskian framework in which this study was carried out, and in which the data from the experimental task will be analyzed. Importantly, this chapter explains Vygotsky's social, discursive and activity-based understanding of consciousness and mental activity, and the role of semiotic (linguistic) mediation in the carrying out of higher mental functions. Chapter 2 also introduces Vygotsky's methodological paradigm, or Genetic Method, in the spirit of which the present study was conducted, and also describes the specific procedures used in the collection of data.

The activity-based linguistic analysis of the recall data is presented in Chapters 3, 4 and 5. Chapters 3 and 4 consider the recalls of L2 (Spanish) and L1 (English) language texts, respectively, and examine the protocols for signs of private writing and other evidence that would suggest that the learners have purposefully availed themselves of external linguistic means in order to complete the task. Chapter 5 draws on the private writing features observed in Chapters 3 and 4, and presents an overall analysis of the learners' activity and, particularly, of their orientation to the experimental task, as suggested by these features and other characteristics of the recall protocols. The analysis presented in Chapter 5 provides further evidence of the mediational properties of written language, and gives support to the claim that tasks do not result in homogenous activity.

1

Text Comprehension and Recall

This chapter presents current assumptions regarding L2 reading comprehension, and introduces the model of reading comprehension and the assessment measure adopted in this study. Several models of text processing (top-down, bottom-up and interactive) will be considered. The present study adopts a version of the interactive model, but exchanges the meaning-extraction view of comprehension assumed under an information processing model for the meaning-construction perspective argued for by Rommetviet (1991, 1992), and Frawley (1987), among others. Finally, this chapter discusses several methods of investigating the reading process and, in light of the constructivist framework adopted, argues in favor of the recall protocol as a means of assessment. It will ultimately be argued that both text comprehension and the production of recall protocols are meaning constructing activities that may, in fact, occur simultaneously.

MODELS OF L2 TEXT COMPREHENSION

In the past two decades, two major models of text comprehension have been put forth, each viewing comprehension from a different and opposing perspective. More recently however, a third, integrated, or interactive, approach has been explored (Bernhardt, 1990, 1991a, 1991b; Carrell, Devine & Eskey, 1988; Grabe, 1991; Lee, 1990; Swaffar, 1988). This section considers the variables involved in text comprehension, presents the interactive model of text comprehension in which these variable are integrated, and discusses this model in light of the fallacy of using a conduit metaphor to explain communication and comprehension (Frawley, 1987; Reddy, 1979).

Text- and Reader-driven Processes in Reading Comprehension

Text comprehension is a complex process in which readers make sense of and attribute an interpretation to a written text. Much of the current reading research is grounded in the computer-based, information-processing model of cognitive science. In this framework, reading is an intrapersonal problem-solving task involving the brain as the central processor, and consisting of a hierarchically ordered series of processes. Thus, instead of being seen as a single, monolithic function, reading is understood as a collection of sub-processes (Bernhardt, 1991a). Traditionally, these processes have been divided into one of two groups: text-driven (also known as bottom-up) and reader-driven (also known as top-down). This dichotomous view of reading reveals the two opposing perspectives from which some researchers approach the problem of reading, that is, from the point of view of the text, or from the point of view of the reader.

Bernhardt (1991a) identifies three types of variables involved in second language reading comprehension: linguistic, literacy, and knowledge factors. Linguistic variables involve essentially text-driven processes, while literacy and knowledge variables represent reader-driven processes (see Bernhardt, 1991b for an extensive review of both text-driven and reader-driven studies). Linguistic processes include those relating to orthography, word recognition, lexicon, syntax, morphology, and text structure, as well as second language proficiency. Literacy processes rely on a reader's operational knowledge about how to approach a text, referring to reading skills independent of language proficiency (Bernhardt, 1991a). Of the three variables, literacy has received the least amount of attention as it is often assumed that literacy skills are constant across populations of sufficient L1 and L2 proficiency. However, two recent studies, Bernhardt and Kamil (1995) and Zwaan and Brown (1996), examining L1 literacy and L2 reading, both find that L1 literacy effects are not constant and, in effect, are mediated by L2 proficiency in L2 reading.

Knowledge processes involve the interpersonal knowledge and experience that readers bring with them to text comprehension. Schema theory puts forth the notion that text processing principally involves the mapping of new information onto already existing and schematically organized background knowledge (Mandler & Johnson, 1977; Kintsch & Greene, 1978). As a result, a large body of L2 reading research focuses on accounting for the role of the reader's background knowledge of content, text structure and cultural factors in text comprehension (c.f. Carrell, 1983; Johnson, 1981; Lee, 1986; Rumelhart, 1980; Steffenson & Joag-Dev, 1984).

In spite of the apparent complexity of text comprehension—and the fact that it involves a number of different processes—the tendency in the research, until recently, has focused almost exclusively on either a text-driven or a reader-driven approach to reading and has addressed the problem of reading by focusing on one process at a time. Much of the literature is divided into text-driven or reader-driven research, all in search of what Bernhardt (1991b) calls the "smoking gun," or that factor which would ultimately account for proficiency in reading. Studies have shown that the processes mentioned above do contribute to reading comprehension. However, Bernhardt (1991b) argues convincingly against a "one factor at a time" approach, criticizing the methodology used in examining variables in isolation, which may, in fact, bias the results towards the individual factors. Additionally, she argues that while some of the generalizations derived from this research may be valid, neither text-driven nor reader-driven variables by themselves have been able to predict reading proficiency to any great degree. Instead, to explain text comprehension, it is necessary to describe and account for both types of processes simultaneously.

Interactive Models

In order to compensate for the shortcomings of the purely text-driven or reader-driven models, most current models of second language reading comprehension are integrative or interactive in nature (c.f. Bernhardt, 1990, 1991a, 1991b; Carrell, Devine & Eskey, 1988; Grabe, 1991; Lee, 1990; Samuels & Kamil, 1984; Swaffar, 1988; Swaffar, Arens & Byner, 1991). As Grabe points out, the term interactive can be used to describe two important and not unrelated characteristics of the reading process. First, the term can refer to the interaction of the various processes, both text-driven and reader-driven, which are involved in text comprehension. Second, the term can refer to the interaction between the reader and the text, as the reader develops a representation of the text, based on the reader's knowledge of the world and the information that she is said to extract from the text.[1]

Neither text-driven nor reader-driven processes have been proven to be a significant predictor of reading comprehension and it is more likely that the different processes work together, influence and support each other during reading (Bernhardt, 1991b). Thus, in interactive models, reading involves the continuous integration of the available information, from both "inside" and "outside" the text, in order to construct a coherent representation of the text. The processes involved are hierarchically structured and interact with each other, providing a constant source of input or information. Bernhardt (1991b) explains:

> The second language reader (as any reader) has perceptual systems working for him
> in addition to phonological, lexical or word meaning, and syntactic processes that
> provide text input. At the same time, the second language reader (as any reader) has
> a knowledge base that fills in the gaps in texts. (p. 120)

Critically, text comprehension is not a linear event, rather, it allows for the reader
to act on former portions of the text in light of new input and to constantly integrate different portions of the text with each other in reconstructing the text.

The integration of input and the interaction of systems works to varying degrees
of success. Bernhardt (1991b), citing Johnston (1983), remarks that the simultaneous operation and integration of the system involves some inherent risks. That
is, if the text is too difficult for the reader (i.e. because she has restricted access to
certain types of information in the text), it is possible that the compensation of one
feature, usually world knowledge, could "cause the reader to build a completely
inappropriate model of text meaning without being aware of the problem"
(Johnston, 1983 cited in Bernhardt, 1991b, p. 120). In that case, the integration
feature of text comprehension only compounds the problem, because it allows the
reader to continue to make inappropriate inferences based on previous ones.

For reading research situated in the information processing tradition, then, text
comprehension involves a number of different processes, all of which seemingly
can function simultaneously. In effect, comprehension is the sum of the cognitive
processes involved in the activity of relating new and incoming information to
information already stored in memory (Bernhardt, 1990, p. 21). The outcome of
this activity is a "comprehension product" or "discourse model." Through the
integration of information extracted from the text and the reader's own background knowledge, the reader interacts with the text and creates a coherent interpretation for the text. Thus, reading is understood as a meaning-extracting process,
by which successful readers are able to extract and interact with the information
contained in the text (Bernhardt, 1991b).

Text Comprehension as Meaning Construction

Proponents of interactive, meaning-extracting perspectives modeled on information processing theory, such as Bernhardt's model outlined above, crucially rely
on the assumption that meaning is contained in texts. The task of the reader, then,
is to extract new information from the text and to integrate it with previous information. The idea that in-coming information needs to be integrated with prior
knowledge (e.g. memory) seems reasonable and will not be opposed here. However, the assumption that meaning can be extracted is strongly challenged by those
who argue that texts themselves do not contain meaning and that reading, instead,
is a meaning-constructing process (Frawley, 1987; Harré & Gillett, 1994). This
constructivist perspective maintains that the meaning-extracting view of the information processing paradigm is a consequence of what Reddy calls the "Conduit

Metaphor," a widely held but inadequate account of the nature of communication (Lakoff & Johnson, 1980; Reddy, 1979). Belief in the Conduit Metaphor is characteristic not only of many areas of linguistics, but also of the way in which language and communication are discussed in everyday contexts in English.

Essentially, the Conduit Metaphor assumes that language is a container of ideas, a "system by which humans package ideas into words" and then send those packages to other people (Frawley, 1987, p. 129). Language is a box into which ideas are put and sent from speaker/writers to hearer/readers. The job of the speaker/writer is to package "real meaning" efficiently into the box. Likewise, the job of the hearer/reader is to open the package, and, in so doing, uncover, or extract, the true meaning.

Such a perspective on communication has numerous repercussions for linguistic inquiry as well as social policy. However, at this point, only those relevant to the present discussion of text comprehension will be explored.[2] For instance, the Conduit Metaphor leads one to believe that there is such a thing as the core meaning of a text, which can then be privileged above other interpretations (Frawley, 1987). Frawley argues, however, that humans do not speak (or write) in terms of real truth, rather in terms of experienced truth—the world as they experience it. Therefore, facts are really only "construed facts" (Frawley, 1987, p. 131).

Texts, nevertheless, are not packages, not even of construed fact. One can not put meaning into texts for they are no more boxes than words are. Frawley (1987) argues that writing a text is an activity of meaning construction that can leave behind, of course, artifacts of the activity such as marks on a page.[3] Rommetveit argues, however, that these marks do not contain meaning, rather, they are simply meaning potentials, relics of a previous, private meaning-construction which may later be actualized for the creation of new meaning (Rommetveit, 1991, 1992). The task of the reader or listener is to construct meaning based on a textual artifact, that is, to actualize those meaning potentials and thus create meaning. Importantly, the construction of meaning is understood to be dialogic and situated. The way in which the hearer/reader will actualize meaning potentials depends on the fixation of "background conditions and perspective" (Rommetveit, 1992, p. 29).

This study rejects the Conduit Metaphor and, following Rommetveit (1991, 1992) and Frawley (1987), replaces it with the notion of meaning potentials (again, a metaphor). Thus, text comprehension is understood as the actualization of this potential in the construction of meaning. Reading, then, is a meaning-making activity. Faced with textual artifacts, readers seek to construct meaning, thus producing an interpretation or representation—in essence a new text—that is accordingly only valid for a given reader and a given text at a given time. Because individual readers form an inherently diverse group, and may themselves be different readers at different times, the individual representations that may be constructed for any one text are necessarily different from each other.

More or less "successful" reading involves building a coherent discourse model by integrating the most important information created for a text into the model.

Implicit in that statement is the idea that not all potential information might find its way into the constructed model. However, that itself is not an indication of imperfect comprehension; text comprehension should not be equated with the ability to produce an identical representation of the original text. Instead, comprehension involves making informed decisions about what is important information, and integrating that information coherently into the growing discourse model. Thus, readers must determine what information is pertinent to understanding the text and decide what to remember of a text, or what to integrate into the model. Different readers will, of course, make different decisions, in part based on their previous knowledge, language proficiency, or personal histories, and thus create different text models. The potential for varied yet equally valid text models is what distinguishes the meaning-construction perspective from the meaning-extracting perspective.

The fact that readers have any decision making power in this whole process implies that they have intentions which play a large role in determining meaning actualization. The critical factor of intentionality is often not accounted for in reading research. Usually, for the sake of controlling variables in the research project, it is regularly assumed that the readers will adopt the intention of the researcher, who is very frequently interested in having the subjects read and comprehend the entire text. However, the reader's intention plays a crucial role in deciding what and how much meaning to actualize. Compare, for example, the case of the scholar who leafs through a new journal article with the intention of keeping up with development in the field with one who reads the same article in the hopes of finding additional support for a specific hypothesis. It is likely that in the two cases the meaning actualization will be different. The first scholar might construct a loosely coherent model touching on all areas of the text, while the second might actualize meaning only where relevant to the discussion of her specific hypothesis. Of course, it is possible that these two fictitious scholars are actually one and the same person, whose intentions have changed over time.[4]

Text comprehension in a constructionist framework, then, like the comprehension of oral discourse, can be understood as the creating and assigning of a unique interpretation to a text, based on lexical, syntactic, and structural clues, as well as background knowledge, intentions, and overall experience of the reader in the world. Comprehension involves the constant integration of newly constructed meaning with previously constructed meaning and prior knowledge, along with the ability to edit the model, that is, to decide which meaning is relevant to the gist of the text and to the intentions of the reader. The association among the variable sources of input, the interaction of the reader with the text and the fact that no two readers are exactly alike in terms of experience, proficiency and intention, all result in an unlimited number of possibilities or "potentialities" in the creation and assignment of meaning to a single text.

ASSESSING READING COMPREHENSION

Recall protocols have been employed throughout the literature as a measure of reading comprehension (c.f. Appel, 1986; Appel & Lantolf, 1994; Bernhardt, 1983, 1987, 1990, 1991a, 1991b; Carrell, 1984a, 1984b, 1985, 1987; Davis, Lange & Samuels, 1988; Floyd & Carrell, 1987 Horiba, 1993; Horiba, van den Broek & Fletcher, 1993; Lee, 1986, 1990; Lee & Riley, 1990; Roller & Matambo, 1992; Steffenson & Joag-Dev, 1984; Urquhart, 1984). The procedure usually involves having subjects recall, either in written or oral mode, everything that they are able remember of the text which they have read, without that text being present. Traditional analyses of protocols are quantitative and attempt to measure the amount of information recalled in relation to the original text. Quantifying comprehension is achieved by breaking the original text in idea units or propositions and checking the recall against this list of idea units (see Bernhardt, 1991b for a discussion of various scoring procedures). Bernhardt (1990, 1991b) and Lee (1986, 1990) employ qualitative analyses, especially of reader error, in an attempt to explain text comprehension by examining those points in the process where readers go astray.

The motivation for using recall protocols comes from the assumption that people can remember what they have understood (Appel & Lantolf, 1994). This implies that the recalled text to some extent ought to reflect the comprehension product. Thus, the protocol offers some information on how the text was reconstructed. By examining the recall protocol, one can see what information was integrated into the reconstruction and how that information was organized (Bernhardt, 1991b).

Ballstaedt and Mandl (1987) argue that open-ended comprehension questions offer a more accurate insight into what the reader has comprehended, citing that the recall protocol is susceptible to the particular writing habits as well as to the motivation of the subjects. However, Bernhardt (1983, 1991b) argues convincingly against the use of questions, both multiple choice and open-ended, as a global assessment measure. In both cases, the structure and content of such questions can constrain the possible answers. This is especially true of the multiple choice test, where the instrument in fact suggests possible answers, and which very often can be answered correctly independent of having read the text (Bernhardt, 1983). Moreover, multiple choice and open-ended questions, because they necessarily deal with the target text, and because they are texts themselves, become additional sources of information, and may cause the reader to alter his or her representation of the text during the procedure. In such a case, Bernhardt argues, the test instrument itself would affect the comprehension product, without providing evidence of its doing so.

Other researchers have argued for on-line assessment, such as think-aloud procedures, proposing that only measures such as these can reveal what is going on at the time of comprehension (Horiba, 1993; Trabasso & Suh, 1993, Trabasso &

Magliano, 1996). However, the use of conscious methods such as introspection and think-alouds to tap unconscious mental behavior is problematic at best; it has yet to be shown that subjects can both perform a cognitive task and report on it without changing or contaminating the task itself in some way (Donato & Lantolf, 1992). Moreover, Bernhardt (1991b) proposes that qualitative analyses of recall protocols can offer insight into the interactive nature of text comprehension. For example, Bernhardt's (1991b) and Lee's (1990) focus on readers' errors and their integration into the reconstructed text, allows the researcher a view of the interaction of the various factors as a reader constructs a representation of a text.

The present study adopts the recall protocol as its assessment measure, largely because the protocol does seem to reflect comprehension, that is, the propositional content of the text reconstruction, as well as the organization of the propositional content. Additionally, and contrary to the assumptions of many, this measure is chosen because recall protocols allow us to observe the possibility of on-going comprehension of the target text. It may seem odd to adopt the recall protocol in order to discover on-line modifications in the discourse model (i.e. continued comprehension), especially since researchers such as Lee and Bernhardt consider protocols to be "cleaner" (or more text dependent) than other measures (such as multiple choice tests, etc.). Indeed, Bernhardt (1991b) argues that, among other reasons, the recall protocol is a good measure precisely because "generating recall data does not influence the reader's understanding of a text" (Bernhardt, 1991b, p. 200).

Implicit in that statement, however, is the assumption that text comprehension can only take place during the actual time of reading and, moreover, that recall protocols reflect only the comprehension product that was elaborated at the time of reading. These assumptions about reading and recall stem from a Conduit Metaphor-based view of language and, in light of our previous discussion, will be rejected here.

To say that comprehension can only take place at the time of reading assumes that the text itself contains meaning. In a constructivist model, however, written texts contain meaning potentials, with which readers may construct meaning, depending on the fixation of certain conditions. It stands to reason, then, that should one of these conditions change, the meaning should also be altered. As Markovà (1992) writing about oral discourse, states:

> Meaning goes beyond the moment the utterance ends. The speaker may "understand backwards" the meaning of what was said, transcending temporality and a sequential structure of messages. [quotes in original] (p. 55)

Kintsch (1993) also argues that inference and elaboration of the actualized meaning may take place both "during and after the original comprehension of a text," in response to certain tasks (p. 198). Thus, the question is not whether comprehension is transformed, but rather what causes it to do so (e.g. the attaining of additional knowledge, an illustration, or even discussion). What is interesting is that Marková, unlike Kintsch, was not referring to text comprehension, but rather to the production of oral discourse, and suggests that speaking in some way facilitates the process of meaning actualization, a possibility that is discussed in more detail below.

The second assumption to be called into question is that the recall protocol reflects only already understood information. Again, such a view is predicated on the notion that producing recall text involves repackaging the original text into words. However, once the Conduit Metaphor has been replaced by the view of text as meaning potential, this can no longer be the case. It has been argued here that text production (speaking, writing) and comprehension (listening, reading) involve the construction of meaning. Thus, producing a recall text involves the creation of a new text (based in part on the discourse model created at the time of reading), rather than simply the repackaging of old information. What is more, the construction of the recall protocol may itself alter the conditions of the text and cause the reader-turned-writer to construct different meaning. Thus, the use of recall protocols does not imply the simple sequence "read the text$j$, construct model$j$, remember or recall model$j$, write model$j$." Rather, meaning is constructed at the time of reading and may be later reconstructed or remembered during the production of a "recall" protocol, spoken or written. However, the construction of further meaning may emerge in the context of writing the protocol, thus ensuring that the reconstructed meaning differs from earlier constructions.

Evidence that this is the case can be found in the Vygotskian analysis of oral recall protocols of L1 and L2 English speakers in Appel (1986) and Appel and Lantolf (1994). Examining the metacomments found in the protocols, Appel and Lantolf argue against the unconditional sequencing of comprehension and recall and instead propose that unfolding speech may serve as comprehension. They encountered metacomments such "I guess that means" and argued that such comments could not have entered into the recall had the comprehension process been completed when the reading ended. Rather, these comments are evidence that comprehension, or meaning-construction, carried over into the activity of "recall" itself.

Additionally, Appel (1986) and Appel & Lantolf (1994) found that the subjects often had not realized that they had not understood the text until they attempted to recall it, a phenomenon they refer to as the "illusion of comprehension." When subjects realized that they had, in fact, not understood the text completely, they tended to externalize the process "of finding and/or creating the appropriate continuation of the text" (Appel, 1986, p. 115). This speech, then, ceased to act as a recall of the text (or reconstruction of previously constructed material), but rather served as a knowing strategy (or the construction of new information) (Appel, 1986). The strategy, then, allowed the subjects to "understand backward," as Marková (1992) might argue, and to continue to actualize meaning potentials.

Thus, producing a recall protocol may be one task that initiates, facilitates, and transforms the ongoing actualization of meaning.

SUMMARY

In this chapter, some of the assumptions adopted in the present study have been laid out. Namely, it has been argued that text comprehension involves the interaction of various processes and the construction of meaning. Both reader-driven and text-driven factors interact with each other and with the reader as she engages in the activity of text comprehension, which is understood here to consist of the actualization of meaning. This meaning-making activity may continue in and indeed be transformed by the activity of producing a recall protocol. The capacity of the recall protocol to reflect ongoing meaning-construction makes this method of assessment a particularly valuable one in the investigation of the mental processes involved in text comprehension.

NOTES

[1]   This second sense of interactive is referred to by Bernhardt, Lee and others as constructivist in the sense that readers put together or construct a representation of the text, based, in part, on the information that they are able to extract from the text (see Bernhardt, 1990, 1991a, 1991b, Grabe, 1991, Lee, 1990). However, this position, very much a product of information processing theory, is fundamentally different from the meaning-making, constructivist perspective that will be put forth in the following sub-section. In order to avoid confusion, Bernhardt's model will not be referred to as constructivist, but rather as interactive.

[2]   See Frawley (1987) for a discussion of some of the social and political consequences of a view of knowledge predicated on the Conduit Metaphor

[3]   Similarly, speaking produces only acoustic vibrations in the air (Frawley, 1987).

[4]   In the same way, one could also consider the intentions of the writer and their role in delimiting how the meaning potentials of given texts would be actualized.

2

A Sociocultural Approach to the Study of Mind

For Vygotsky, an explanation of consciousness is the overriding goal of psychology. However, in attempting to discover the properties of the mind, Vygotsky did not limit his investigation to some isolated, abstract realm. Rather, he opened up the problem of consciousness to include both language and behavior, arguing that it was impossible to explain consciousness without taking language into account. He advocated this approach, not because he thought that language in itself could somehow shed light on the problem of consciousness, but because he felt that thought and language were part of a unified phenomenon. Thus, Vygotsky endeavored to investigate the mind as it is realized linguistically in activity, placing particular importance on the role of the sociocultural milieu in shaping both the language and the activity. That being the case, it is more accurate to say that the relevant domain of inquiry for Vygotsky was that of psycholinguistics.

To say that Vygotsky was a psycholinguist requires some clarification, in light of the fact that the study of psycholinguistics in the West has seen the rise of three distinct theoretical paradigms or, to use Mehler and Noizet's (1973) taxonomy, generations (in A. A. Leontiev, 1981). The first generation was the Behaviorist or Neo-Behaviorist school, in which language was more or less reduced to reaction to physical and verbal stimuli. The Behaviorists, represented in the work of Osgood and Sebeok (1965) were clearly oriented toward psychology, itself conceived as a system of behavioral processes, leaving aside, for the most part, the question of language. Second generation psycholinguistics was part of the new cognitive science expounded by Miller and Johnson-Laird (1976), and influenced by Chomsky's syntactic theory (1972). This paradigm focuses almost entirely on the rules which regulate the structure of language, or more precisely, the sentence. Second generation psycholinguistics says little about psychological processes, which are deemed inaccessible and are essentially reduced to mere speech manifestations of linguistic structure (A. A. Leontiev, 1981).

Third generation psycholinguistics, first evident in the work of Bruner (1973) and Blakar and Rommetveit (1975), has also been called the second cognitive revolution (Harré & Gillett, 1994). This psycholinguistic paradigm departs from its predecessors most significantly in that it treats psychological and linguistic processes as a unified phenomenon. The focus of investigation shifts from an analysis of abstract speech processes to a psychological analysis of speech and thought (A. N. Leontiev, 1981). Moreover, this approach emphasizes utterance or discourse, as opposed to idealized sentences, taking into account the sociocultural context. In the West, this approach is known as Discursive (Harré & Gillett, 1994), Sociotextual (Frawley, 1987), Dialogical (Rommetviet, 1991, 1992; Wold, 1992b) and Sociocultural (Wertsch, 1985b, 1991) Psycholinguistics.

It is not until the emergence of the third generation of psycholinguistics in the late 1970s, then, that Vygotsky would have been considered a psycholinguist in the West. This is profoundly ironic, of course, given that Vygotsky died in 1934. His ideas had not lain fallow, however. Rather, they served as the basis of Speech-activity Theory that was further developed by scholars such as A. N. Leontiev, A. A. Leontiev, Galperin, Luria, and others.

The first English language version of "Thought and Language" was published in 1962, and Soskin and John's (1963) seminal work on private speech appeared the following year. Nonetheless, Vygotsky's ideas did not begin to attract much attention in the West until the work of Scribner and Cole (1973, 1981) and Wertsch (1981a, 1985a, 1985b), which has been instrumental in introducing Sociocultural (or Sociohistorical) Theory to Western researchers. Both Speech-activity Theory and its Western offspring, Sociocultural Theory, have greatly contributed to the further development and enrichment of third generation psycholinguistics.

Sociocultural Theory is a theory of mind, based on Vygotsky's belief that the properties of the mind can be discovered by observing mental, physical, and linguistic activity, because they are intrinsically related. Thus, it is the very nature of mind that compels us not only to make reference to language in a theory of consciousness, but essentially to consider language and consciousness as a single problem. It is in this sense that Vygotsky was a psycholinguist.

This chapter outlines the Sociocultural approach to the study of mind and addresses two crucial questions: What is the nature of consciousness and under which circumstances can it be investigated.[1] The first section of this chapter proposes that consciousness is mental activity as it is organized through semiotic, namely linguistic, means. The second section discusses Vygotsky's claim that consciousness can be objectively observed in mental and physical behavior. This section introduces the concept of activity as the explanatory principle for consciousness and outlines the Theory of Activity as first suggested by Vygotsky and later developed by A.N. Leontiev and others. The role of language in the execution of activity is also discussed. The third section of this chapter focuses on a particular mental activity, that of self-regulation. The need to self-regulate is present in all other activity, which has led some to propose that ultimately the purpose of consciousness is to order and control itself through language (Frawley, 1987). This section discusses regulation and regulative strategies employed by individuals when self-regulation is difficult to achieve or maintain. Special attention will be given to the language which mediates self-regulation, known as private speech or private writing, and its distinctive linguistic features, as discovered in research carried out in the Sociocultural framework. The fourth and final section of this chapter outlines Vygotsky's methodological framework, specifically his genetic method, and describes the motives and procedures behind the present study.

CONSCIOUSNESS AND SYMBOLIC MEDIATION

Vygotsky believed that understanding consciousness ought to be the ultimate goal of psychology. Nonetheless, he found himself at odds with the two dominant, yet incompatible, psychological paradigms of his day. He went so far, in fact, as to refer to the state of affairs as "the crisis in psychology", rejecting both the behaviorist model and the subjective-idealist approach (Vygotsky, 1986, p. 13). The behaviorist approach proposed that the study of human psychology could be reduced to the study of reflexes—essentially excluding consciousness from the analysis (Wertsch, 1985b). The idealist approach, on the other hand, considered psychology to be an entirely subjective affair in which consciousness could only be studied through non-objective methods, such as introspection.

It was in the notion of activity that Vygotsky found the basis of his initial attempts to explain consciousness.[2] Largely ignored in Western psychology until the late 1970s, activity has long been at the center of Soviet psychological research. The roots of activity as a psychological concept trace back to the philosophical writings of Spinoza, Marx, Engels, and Lenin, and, most notably, to Marx's *Sixth Thesis on Feuerbach*. Vygotsky, however, recurred to the notion of activity in order to procure what he felt was most lacking from the psychological discussions of his day: an acceptable definition of consciousness.

Vygotsky's response to the dilemma was to introduce the notion of consciousness into an objective approach, arguing that consciousness was "the objectively observable organization of behavior" (Wertsch, 1985b, p.187). According to Vygotsky, the essence of consciousness is the way in which humans constantly construct their environment and its representation by engaging in various forms of activity (Wertsch, 1985b, p. 188). Essentially, consciousness is a process, a mental activity in which sociocultural meaning is constructed in the wider context of human activity, that is, the business of living.[3]

For Vygotsky, consciousness did not exist prior to human experience but because of it. This position was summed up by A. N. Leontiev (1981), who stated that consciousness does not underlie life, rather "life underlies consciousness" (p. 57). Consciousness, then, arises out of the way in which humans organize their lives, their psychological and physical activity. Vygotsky saw consciousness as the way in which people dynamically structure and realize higher mental functions such as voluntary attention, voluntary memory, intention, planning, and the resulting physical behavior.[4] This organization is not, as cognitive scientists in the Cartesian tradition would argue, a preexisting, underlying system of abstract representations that determine our behavior. Rather, Vygotsky argues that behavior and consciousness arise and exist together. Therefore, consciousness may be observed in the organization of human behavior.

Vygotsky was interested in the organizational properties of consciousness, specifically, in how mental processes are structured and executed. To solve this problem, he drew again on Marxist philosophy, this time on the political and social writings of Engels, who stressed the importance of physical tools in mediating and controlling objects in the physical environment. Vygotsky analogized this concept to the case of consciousness, where both the activity and the tools are psychological and argued that the most powerful psychological tool is an elaborate semiotic system, that is, language. Vygotsky observed that language was crucially relevant to the problem of consciousness:

> The problem of speaking and speech belongs to the set of psychological problems in which the main issue is the relationship among various psychological functions, among the various forms of the activity of consciousness. (Cited in Wertsch 1985b, p. 195)

In the case of mental activity, Vygotsky argued that it was the word, or more precisely word meaning, which was crucially involved in the dynamic organization of consciousness. The role of symbolic mediation in consciousness was also observed by Wittgenstein (1953), who stated that "thinking is the activity of operating with signs" (cited in Harré & Gillett, 1994, p. 50).

It should be pointed out that by word meaning Vygotsky did not only allude to the referential meaning (*znachenie*) of individual words, as has often been argued, but also to the sense (*smysl*) of a word, that is, "the aggregate of all the psychological facts emerging in our consciousness because of this word" (Vygotsky, 1934, cited in Wertsch, 1995b, p. 196). Furthermore, given Vygotsky's long-standing interest in the development of mental functions, it becomes apparent that he also referred to the formation of concepts and the important role of language as the tool that mediates concept formation. Thus, in Sociocultural Theory, consciousness, or higher mental activity, is the creation of meaning through the manipulation of symbols, as directed at a goal and arising from a motive.

At no point did Vygotsky propose an isomorphic relationship between thought and language. However, he did argue that language mediates thought to such a large degree that higher thought ought to be impossible without language (Frawley, 1987). Most importantly, Vygotsky (1986) claimed that thought is completed in language.

Vygotsky's original ideas about semiotic mediation have been extended considerably by the speech-activity theorists in the former Soviet Union (A. N. Leontiev, A. A. Leontiev, Luria) as well as by researchers in the West such as Scribner and Cole (1973, 1981), Kozulin (1986, 1990), Wertsch (1985b, 1991), Frawley (1987), and Harré and Gillett (1994). Harré and Gillett argue that it is not merely the individual word or concept that makes up consciousness, but rather it is the discourse. Similarly, Frawley proposes that mind is a sociotextual process. These analysis are alike in that they see mind as a discursive process. The emphasis on discourse unites the essential features of mind as originally proposed by Vygotsky and as currently explained by Sociocultural researchers in third-generation psycholinguistics: consciousness implies language or symbol use, process, and activity in social space.

First, the notion of discourse reinforces Vygotsky's idea that mental activity is made up of "individual and private uses of symbolic systems" (Harré & Gillett 1994, p. 27). Also, like Vygotsky, discursive psychology emphasizes that consciousness is mental activity achieved through discourse, whether public or private, and not underlying or hidden abstract processes. Harré and Gillett write of mental activity:

> [f]or example, acts of remembering are not manifestations of hidden subjective, psychological phenomena. They *are* the psychological phenomena. Sometimes they have subjective counterparts; sometimes they do not [...] There is no necessary shadow world of mental activity behind discourse in which one is working things out in private [emphasis added]. (p. 27)

Finally, the notion of discourse or sociotextual activity embodies the socioculturally embedded nature of mind and the symbolic system. It situates speakers and thinkers in social, historical, political, cultural and interpersonal contexts. On one hand, this means that mind is realized in the act of discourse—private or public. On the other, this means that mental activity, the operation of a symbolic system, is to a large extent determined by the sociocultural history of the person and the discourses to which she has access. Mind is, then, a symbolically organized social construction, determined by and, thus, visible in, discourse (Harré & Gillett 1994, p. 86).

The Theory of Activity

Vygotsky argued against the behaviorist and idealist models of his day, not only on the basis of their definition of consciousness, but also because of the ways in which they attempted to investigate the phenomenon. He rejected both the subjective introspection of the idealist methods and the objective, reflex-oriented methodology of behaviorism. Vygotsky was especially critical of both schools because he felt their methods failed to distinguish between the object of study and the explanatory principle, and thus were both caught up in a rather vicious circle: They were not able to explain anything without making reference to the object of study.

Vygotsky argued that if consciousness were to be the object of study, then some other layer of reality should be referred to in the course of the explanation (Kozulin 1990, p. 83). Thus, he endeavored to discover the most adequate unit of analysis (to be explained below) and the explanatory principal with which to understand consciousness. The insistence on an explanatory principal reflects Vygotsky's goal of explaining human physical and mental behavior, rather than merely describing or even predicting it. He felt that the methodology of the natural sciences was inappropriate for the understanding of mental behavior, since it tended to treat subjects as inert objects (Lantolf & Appel, 1994, p. 23). Therefore, Vygotsky was looking for a framework in which the essence of human action could be observed and understood on its own terms, as well as a corresponding unit of analysis.

Once again, Vygotsky turned to the concept of activity, this time for an analytical framework for observing and investigating consciousness. Drawing on his claim that consciousness was the organization of human mental and physical behavior, he proposed that the way to observe consciousness was through its functioning, or activity. In other words, consciousness is the object of study, while activity is the level from which it can be observed. Activity, then, is the explanatory principle for consciousness and all psychological behavior, including linguistic behavior. This line of thinking was significantly expanded on by subsequent scholars, such as A. N. Leontiev (1981) and others, as will be discussed shortly.

A unit of analysis refers to the division of the object of study into analyzable segments. Vygotsky, recognizing the functional unity of consciousness, was adamant in his belief that it could not be studied by reducing it to its component parts. He argued that no single aspect of consciousness could be studied without taking into consideration the remaining aspects (Wertsch,1985b). To do otherwise, Vygotsky insisted, would destroy the object of study itself, since it would necessarily result in products that no longer contained properties of the whole (Lantolf & Appel, 1994; Wertsch 1985b). Drawing an analogy with chemistry, Vygotsky argued that an attempt to study consciousness by teasing it apart into its component elements would be as misleading as trying to study the properties that compose water by breaking it down into hydrogen and oxygen (Wertsch, 1985b). Although water extinguishes fire, the elements of water do not share this property, as hydrogen can ignite, and oxygen, as is known, sustains fire.

Instead of analyzing consciousness as elements, then, Vygotsky proposed analyzing it into units, making an important distinction between the two segments. Unlike an element, a unit is a microcosm which retains the basic properties of the whole, in this case, consciousness. Vygotsky believed that word meaning was crucial to the ordering of consciousness, and therefore was uniquely able to reflect the interfunctional and semiotic organization of mind (Wertsch 1985b). Thus, Vygotsky argued that word meaning was the correct unit of analysis for the study of consciousness and the meaning-making that it entails.[5] Similarly, Harré & Gillett (1994) Frawley (1987), and Rommetveit (1992) look to linguistically constructed social discourse in their investigation of mind.

Features of Activity

Wertsch (1981b) outlines six basic features of activity, three of which are central to the present discussion. First, activity can be analyzed at three distinct levels, that of activity, action, and operation, which correspond to motive, goal, and the conditions of psychological behavior. These distinctions were originally proposed by A. N. Leontiev (1981), and allow the researcher to "examine a single segment of behavior from a variety of viewpoints" (Wertsch, 1981b, p. 18). The second feature, emphasis on goal-directedness, follows from the three-leveled approach to activity, but places special importance on the second level, that of action. The third feature is that of mediation. As explained earlier, semiotic mediation played a central role in Vygotsky's thinking. He argued that symbolic mediation is always present in higher forms of mental activity, (e.g. attention, voluntary memory), and that certain kinds of mediation make possible new and unforeseen types of activity.[6]

The three remaining features, not directly relevant to the present discussion, are genetic explanation, social interaction and appropriation through imitation.[7] The first of these three captures Vygotsky's emphasis on development at various levels—phylogenetic, ontogenetic, microgenetic, and sociohistorical. Social interaction and appropriation both deal with the development of different forms of mediated activity, which arise first in social interaction, and are eventually appropriated by the individual.[8]

The Levels of Activity

Vygotsky's ideas on activity were pursued and expanded upon by a small group of his students, but it was A. N. Leontiev who proposed the three-level analysis of activity. It is important to bear in mind, however, that the notion of levels does not imply that activity is reducible to the levels or the features therein. Again, Vygotsky's anti-reductionist stance is reflected in A. N. Leontiev (1981) who proposed that "activity is the nonadditive, molar unit of life" (p. 46). Nonetheless, the levels provide a macrostructure for considering activity (and, ultimately, consciousness) and units, or viewpoints, from which it can be analyzed. Naturally, then, these levels retain the characteristic properties of the activity as a whole. They proceed from more to less global, and each is associated with a specific type of unit (Wertsch 1985b). Wertsch describes the macrostructure of activity in the following way (see Figure 2.1).

Activity - Motive
Action - Goal
Operations - Condition

FIGURE 2.1.

Before discussing the first level, it must be made clear that A. N. Leontiev and other researchers employ the word activity to refer to two different concepts. The first sense of the word, which is the one used up until now, is broader, and refers in general to the Theory of Activity. This sense must be distinguished from the second, which constitutes the first and highest level of analysis within the theory.

As the highest level of analysis, activity refers to specific human behavior, as this occurs in socioculturally defined contexts. Crucially, A. N. Leontiev (1981) insisted that activity was not determined by mere physical surroundings. Instead, it is the sociocultural setting in which activity takes place that determines the appropriate properties of the activity. The concept of motive is intrinsically linked to activity, since activity is always undertaken in order to satisfy some need. Indeed, A. N. Leontiev (1981) argued that without motive as a driving force, there would be no activity. Thus, all activity comes about as the result of an intention to act, whether a motive is apparent or not. A. N. Leontiev held that it is possible that a motive be concealed or even overlooked in some way. Nonetheless, it is always present. As in the case of activity, motives are also socioculturally and contextually determined. For example, some people have financial motives for learning a second language (i.e. they hope get a better job) while others engage in the activity because it is a requirement.

The second level in the macrostructure of activity involves the two inseparable concepts of action and goal. Actions, according to A. N. Leontiev (1981), are the "basic components" of activities which "translate them into reality" (p. 59). Crucially, actions are goal-directed, performed in order to achieve certain goals. Goals, in turn, follow from motives and one might say, in fact, that motives, which can be general, are operationalized as specific goals (i.e. the general motive "hunger" can potentially be operationalized as the specific goal of eating something).

At this point it might be helpful to give an example of the units discussed thus far, in order to illustrate the concepts as well as demonstrate the dynamic relationship between them. Consider, then, the game of Monopoly™, as an example of a sociohistorically determined activity.[9] There are, of course, a theoretically infinite number of motives for why one might chose to engage in the activity of playing Monopoly™. They include the desire to engage in competitive behavior, to spend time with one's friends or family, and so on.[10] The point is, there must be a reason, or a motive, for engaging in this behavior even if it is clandestine.

The various motives suggested above can be operationalized as immediate goals, such as to win the game, to the lose game, or to simply keep the game going enjoyably for an indefinite length of time, in which case the goal is neither to win nor lose, but just to play. Of course, different players will have different goals. Various actions, such as the throwing of dice, the advancement of game tokens, and the making of decisions, can all be taken in order to achieve these goals. The goal-directed nature of the actions dictates that the individual's goal will determine the actions involved. However, this is not to say that there is a a one to one correspondence between action and goal. Rather, it is well known that the same goal can be achieved through different actions. Potentially, one can achieve the goal of winning the game through different and even opposing strategies, such as playing conservatively versus playing adventurously. Likewise, the same action may be used to achieve different goals. For example, selling off one's property may provide the necessary capital to get oneself out of jail, or it may be a way of allowing a less capable (novice) opponent to participate more fully in the game.

It should become clear from this discussion that even an activity as banal or as unimportant as playing a board game involves a number of different subgoals, which may be subordinated to a higher goal. For example, the goal of winning may involve, in the case at hand, the achieving of a chain of numerous subgoals, such as accumulating a large quantity of wealth at the expense of others, which in turn may involve the subgoal of purchasing property and avoiding Boardwalk, all of which can be reduced to the subgoal of advancing one's game token, a goal that is often achieved through the action of rolling dice.

The third and final level of activity deals with operations and the associated conditions under which they are carried out. Unlike actions, operations are not directed at conscious goals. Rather they are "triggered by the contextual conditions of the task" (Wertsch, 1979, p. 88). Thus, the crucial difference between actions and operations lies in the notion of goal-directedness. Actions are processes focused on the completion of specific goals. Operations, on the other hand, are only loosely connected with the goal, and are more closely related to the material circumstances or conditions under which the goal is to be achieved. An additional difference is that while actions represent conscious and purposeful human functioning, operations are for the most part automatic and determined by present conditions.

The distinction between an action and an operation is not absolute. Rather, whether a function is an action or an operation depends entirely on the individual, the activity and the material circumstances under which the activity is to be carried out. A. N. Leontiev (1981) illustrates this point clearly with the example of shifting gears in an automobile. When initially learning how to shift, the process may involve efforts which are consciously goal-directed. That is, an action may be required. For the inexperienced driver, the goal of driving a car to a specified location implies the subgoal of learning to shift the gear into first, second and so on. After a period of time, the shifting of gears becomes automatic and, therefore, no goal-directed action is involved. The shifting of gears is no longer a goal in and of itself, and instead becomes part of the material circumstances of driving a car. Likewise, shifting into first is no longer an action, but merely a routinized operation connected with the goal of moving the car from point A to point B.

It should also be pointed out that the transition from action to operation is not permanent nor unidirectional. A person for whom shifting is an operation under normal circumstances may very well find herself in a situation where the shifting of gears requires some goal-directed action, such as attention. For example, this may happen initially while driving a car whose clutch is somewhat different, or which has a different number of gears. In this way, whether a function is an action or a operation is situationally defined, depending entirely on the individual, the task and the context.

In summary, the three level macrostructure proposed by Leontiev—activity and motive, actions and goals, and operations and conditions—provides us with an analytic framework for understanding consciousness. The key to explaining activity lies not in considering these units in isolation nor in exaggerating their distinctiveness. Rather it is to be found in understanding the levels as equitable parts of a dynamic, functional system, within which the characteristic properties of the activity can be found at all levels, and whose intersubstitutability does not diminish the indispensability of each unit (Luria, 1973).

Features of Actions

It has been argued that activity can be analyzed in terms of different, yet interrelated and indispensable, units. It is nonetheless the case that the unit of action has been the subject of further elaboration. This may have been based on A. N. Leontiev's somewhat preferential treatment of that unit. Indeed, he refers to action as that basic component of activity that is able to transform activity into reality. Actions, energized by motives and directed toward internal, individual goals, lie at the center of activity.

Still adhering to the macrostructure proposed by A. N. Leontiev (1981) for activity, Galperin and his student, Talyzina, are responsible for a comprehensive elaboration of the level of action, distinguishing between three functional components: orientation, execution and control (Talyzina, 1981). This analysis fits into the three level analysis of activity, and allows the researcher to study how an action is carried out.

The three components do not represent any kind of sequence. Instead, all three are present simultaneously in an action (Talyzina, 1981). The orienting component provides a structural basis for the action. In essence, it is the planning stage of an action, relating the possibility of an action with an assessment of the objective conditions necessary for successful completion of the immediate goal. It is at this point that one takes the proposed activity into consideration, determines what means are available and decides what strategies or actions must be employed in order to achieve success.

The second component of an action is the executive component. This component represents the actual realization of the action. Talyzina (1981) refers to the execution as the "working part of an action" (p. 63). The final component is control, which is concerned with monitoring the planning and executive components of the action. Monitoring the progression of an action allows for the possibility of making corrections to the other two components. Thus, based on the findings of the control component, adjustments may be made to both the orienting and execution component. For example, monitoring may result in a reassessment of the means available and the means necessary for success. Changes in the orienting component may then lead to alterations in the execution.

It is important to point out that the process of completing an action, as realized in its components, is mediated by language, whether vocally or subvocally.[11] This whole process can be illustrated with a example taken from a typical second language classroom. Imagine that the instructor has just asked a question of the class. A student believes that she has the answer, the necessary condition for the achievement of her goal "answer the question correctly." However, as the student begins to speak, she realizes that she does not know all the necessary words in the target language. That is, she comes to know what she does (or does not) know through speaking, and this case, realizes that she cannot go on as originally planned. Thus momentarily reorienting herself to the subgoal of finding the right words, she delays the execution of her intended action and implements, instead, a lexical search, either vocalized or subvocalized. However, still monitoring the situation, she realizes that she cannot come up with the right word. She formulates and weighs several possible ways to continue in the activity (e.g. to stop, ask for help, use the native language) and implements one of them.

Activity and Task

Human activity, as has been shown, is a complex process, analyzable from different levels and involving different units such as motive, goal, action, and orientation. The properties of any given activity are determined by the sociohistorical setting and by the individual. Thus, the phenomenon of shifting gears is an appropriate activity in an environment where the driving of automobiles is frequent behavior for some people of a certain age. As a segment of human activity, shifting may be an operation for experienced drivers in optimal conditions, a goal-directed action for novice drivers, and perhaps even an activity for the quality control specialist at the automobile factory whose job is to test the vehicles. For those who choose to drive cars with automatic transmissions, one can argue, shifting gears is no longer an appropriate or motivated activity, and in fact, ceases to exist.

The fluidity between components of activity, entirely context-dependent and unforeseenably dynamic, is what makes each segment of human functioning unique. In other words, no activity is quite like any other. Thus, driving the car to the nearest store is not the same activity for the novice driver as for the experienced driver, because their shifting activity differs at the level of goal-directedness. Even for two experienced drivers, one could not say that the activity is the same, given the likelihood that the motives or the goals of each are different.

Bearing in mind, then, the complex and multivariate nature of human activity, it is appropriate to consider the concept of task in the context of language learning. An analysis of task from within the investigative framework of activity theory ought to shed light on current definitions of task as formulated with regard to second language acquisition. Drawing on empirical evidence and arguments from Coughlin and Duff (1994), it will be shown that tasks are not predictable segments of human functioning, in spite of the wishes of instructors and researchers to the contrary.

The notion of task has come into popularity in second language teaching and research only in the last decade, following the advent of a discipline-wide focus on communicative language teaching. Tasks are used in the classroom as a teaching practice and as a research method in classroom and experimental situations. (Crookes & Gass 1993a, 1993b). In principle, tasks are designed to promote activity in which language learners are given the opportunity to use language as a tool of communication rather than to focus on linguistic structure. Nunan (1989) writes that a task is:

> a piece of classroom work which involves learners in comprehending, manipulating, producing or interacting in the target language while their attention is primarily focused on meaning rather than form. (p. 10)

In some instances, the concept of task has been restricted to so-called "real-world" tasks. These are tasks which attempt to approximate language functions and communicative interactions which the learner would be likely to engage in outside of classroom (Crookes & Gass, 1993b). These sorts of tasks promote interaction in which learners are able to practice functions of language at the same time as they develop their own linguistic systems. Nunan (1989, p. 38) argues, however, that even tasks that do not replicate "real-world" behavior are valid as long as they help learners to "develop the skills that they will need for carrying out real-world communicative tasks beyond the classroom."

Tasks are often used in experimental research in order to elicit performance data from subjects. Because they are believed to be controllable and measurable, tasks have earned the status of a constant in research design (Coughlin & Duff 1994, p. 174). However, Coughlin and Duff (1994) argue that the behavior found in experimental conditions is neither constant nor controllable. The reason for this is that behavior on task is best understood as activity.

Coughlin and Duff (1994) distinguish clearly between task and activity and argue that tasks are merely "behavior blueprints," motivated by the researcher's agenda (or the teacher's plan) and imposed on learners. In comparison, activity is the

> behavior that is actually produced when an individual (or group) performs a task. It is the process, as well as the outcome of the task, examined in its sociocultural context. (Coughlin & Duff 1994, p. 175)

Thus, task and activity are both part of experimental and instructional conditions. The task represents what the researcher (or the instructor) would like the learner to do, and activity is what the learner actually does. That is, activity is how learners construct the task.

It has been argued that activity is a complex process and that each occasion of activity differs between and within individuals. That being the case, then, task performance, if understood as activity, can neither be constant nor controlled. Coughlin and Duff illustrate this through a comparison of across-learner and within-learner performance on a standard picture description task. They find that in each case, the task yields visibly different activity, which they attribute to small, yet important, differences in the material circumstances of the activity, as well as in the learners' perception of, or orientation to, the conditions of the task. Specifically, Coughlin and Duff discovered that some of the differences might have arisen from the on-going struggle experienced by the learners, as they attempted to realize an anti-social and contrived experimental task in the presence of another person, namely, the researcher.

The role of orientation in determining task performance is one commonly overlooked by social science researchers in general. It is often assumed that subjects will simply adopt the orientation prescribed by the researcher. However, orientation is, like the other features of activity, contextually derived, one crucial part of the context being the individual herself. Thus, it is practically impossible for a researcher to pass on an orientation (usually in the form of directions for completing the task) to the subject. The necessary discrepancy between the orientation of the researcher and that of the subject is a major reason why task performance—activity—is not predictable.

Thus, experimental tasks do not elicit the controlled behavior that one might like. Tasks are behavior blueprints, or, to borrow from Rommetveit (1991, 1992), activity potentials. This is, of course, not only true of experimental conditions but of all imposed tasks. Tasks, or behavior blueprints, exist in many forms. For example, it is commonplace in some language classrooms to require students to learn (or at least briefly memorize) large amounts of second language vocabulary. That requirement is often operationalized as the students' well-defined goal of successfully completing the vocabulary section on the chapter quizzes. However, the actions taken to achieve this goal may differ across learners, depending on each individual's orientation, motivation, personal history, material circumstances (such as time), or some other aspect of the activity. Some students make flashcards or study sheets in an effort to internalize native/second language lexical pairs. Others may take recourse to different mnemonic or even visual devices. Still others may come to the quiz, without prior activity directed at this goal, prepared to make use of their knowledge of other, related languages. Finally, for those who absent themselves from class on the day of the quiz, the activity is realized as not completing, or at least postponing, the task.[12] In this way a single blueprint can generate a multitude of activity. It can be said then, that there are standardized tasks, but there is no standardized activity.

This discussion is not meant to imply that task- generated data is useless in the line of psychological inquiry. On the contrary, such data is potentially quite revealing, as long as it is treated as an instance of realized activity potential, and not simply as a monolithic-like performance on a standardized task. In much second language research it is necessary, for the purpose of the experiment, to assume that learners are homogenous individuals engaged in the same activity (i.e. doing the same thing) in compliance with the wishes of the researchers. Often the suggestion that this not be the case threatens the supposed validity of the test instrument and the experiment itself, or causes certain learners to be removed from the study. However, investigation pursued in the framework of Activity Theory is not threatened in this way, because it anticipates, and thus has the potential to explain, task-generated activity in a principled and theoretical way. Since symbolic mediation is the organizational principle of active meaning-making, one way of investigating and explaining mental functioning is through an examination and analysis of the language activity that tasks generate. Such an analysis, for example, allows the investigator insight into how learners orient themselves to the task and how that orientation affects the execution and control of the activity, thus revealing more about the dynamic and complex nature of consciousness. This method of investigation, particularly as it relates to the study of a specific mental activity, self-regulation, will be elaborated on in the following section.

REGULATION AND MEDIATION

It has been argued, then, that consciousness is essentially a discursive act, the linguistically mediated organization of activity in a particular sociocultural context. This section will now turn to a specific psychological activity, namely, that of regulation and the way in which language mediates the ongoing struggle to attain and maintain self-regulation.

Self-regulation and Private Speech

Regulation refers to control over the self. It is a mental activity which was of vital interest to Vygotsky's thinking. Again, it is clear that Vygotsky was borrowing from the ideas of Engels, who argued that human (physical) activity seeks to control and transform the environment. Likewise, Vygotsky argued that a crucial psychological function was that of controlling and transforming the self. The cognitive activity of achieving and maintaining regulation is inherently tied to all other psychological and physical behavior, in the sense that it is in the context of performing other activities that humans seek to regulate themselves.

Wertsch has identified three forms of regulation, which are defined by the locus of control. Sociocultural Theory proposes that child development is, in large part, the evolution of self-regulation out of other forms of regulation, unfolding in the following order: object- regulation, other-regulation, and self-regulation (Wertsch, 1979). Object-regulation refers to the situation in which all activity is suggested by the environment. In this case, children can only respond to what is in their immediate surroundings. At this point, they have not developed the cognitive skills necessary to perform certain actions by themselves. Instead of planning and executing an action, then, they are limited to "describing and naming certain aspects of the action and environment" (Wertsch, 1979, p. 93). In other-regulation, control of a child's actions lies in the voice of an other who directs the activity. In this way the child is able to complete the required actions. In self-regulation, the child is capable of controlling her own activity and the environment.

Vygotsky argued that the attainment of self-regulation and other higher psychological functions involves the appropriation of external regulation (other- and object- regulation) (Wertsch, 1985b). Vygotsky, unlike Piaget, proposed that all developmental functions such as regulation arise first on the social or interpsychological plane, and then on the individual or intrapsychological plane (Vygotsky, 1986). Initially, regulation is social; adults or other more capable persons direct the child's activity by means of gestures or speech. The adult guides the child through tasks or directs her attention. In the transition to the individual plane, when children first attempt to take control of those same processes, they do so following the model provided to them by semiotically constituted interaction with others. That is, they try to regulate their own behavior via speech. Although it is vocalized, this speech is not speech with communicative purposes. Rather it is speech for the self, or private speech.[13] Private speech allows children to plan, direct and evaluate their behavior. Thus, as in the case of other higher psychological functions, regulation is mediated by language. Language helps to plan and carry out the mental task of regulating the self. In fact, Vygotsky (1986) argued that it was precisely in this context of self-regulation that thinking and speech converge.

Piaget, finding abundant examples of speech for the self in his work with children, argued that egocentric speech was merely a by-product of the child's activity, and reflected the child's early egocentrism and lack of socialization (Vygotsky, 1986). Sociocultural Theory, however, maintains that private speech is not an epiphenomenon. Rather, the emergence of such speech represents the transfer of psychological processes from the interpsychological to the intrapsychcholgical plane and is evidence that self regulation is developing. In his experiments, Vygotsky (1986) found that the amount of private speech in children almost doubled when faced with a difficult task. He argued, then, that private speech arose in an attempt to resolve problems. Vygotsky (1986), describing one experiment, explained that:

> The child would try to grasp and to remedy the situation in talking to himself: "Where's the pencil? I need a blue pencil. Never mind. I'll draw with the red one and wet it with water; it will become dark and look like blue." (p. 30)

Private speech, initially, as shown by the example above, is communicative in form although not in function. In that way, private speech may resemble a dialogue or a conversation with the self, supporting Vygotsky's claim that the origin of private speech is social. Eventually, private speech becomes more abbreviated until it consists mostly of predicative speech or new information (Wertsch, 1979). Ultimately, private speech "goes underground" and evolves into inner (non-vocalized) speech.

The development of self-regulation from other- and object-regulation, as well as the evolution of social speech to inner speech should not be understood as being strictly linear. That is, while Sociocultural Theory proposes that the development of higher psychological processes follows an ordered sequence along an inward path, it is important to keep in mind that self-regulation is, as Frawley and Lantolf (1985) explain, "a relative phenomenon" and can reflect a host of individual differences (p. 20). That is, an individual child may be self-regulated with regard to a certain task, but will rely on other-regulation to accomplish other tasks. At the same time, it may be that:

> a child of four will have achieved self-regulation in a given task while another child, of the same age, will require other-regulation to solve the task. What is more, an older child may be other-regulated in the same task. (Frawley & Lantolf, 1985, p. 20)

Additionally, it must not be assumed that adults are absolutely self-regulated. While adults are, for the most part, able to function in a largely autonomous manner, they often find themselves being other- or object-controlled in difficult situations (Frawley & Lantolf, 1985). The externalization of cognitive processes is not uncommon in adults, even though they have achieved the internalization of higher mental functions (John-Steiner, 1992). Rather, self-regulating inner speech often re-emerges as private speech when adults are confronted with a cognitively challenging task (DiCamilla & Lantolf, 1994). This possibility is explained by the principle of "continuous access," which maintains that adults are able to re-access previous regulating strategies used to develop competence in other domains (Frawley & Lantolf, 1985, p. 22).

Private speech in adults, then (as in children) is speech that emerges when the locus of control is outside the individual, and has the intention of establishing self-regulation. In his studies of private speech in children, Vygotsky considered only self-directed utterances. However, Frawley (1992) has argued that the definition of private speech should be broadened to include all speech for self, whether it be the self-directed remark or in the guise of communicative speech. That is, even speech that is apparently communicative in nature may be private, in that it reflects a lack of control and an attempt to regain self-regulation.

Vygotsky was concerned with the structure and content of inner speech. He did not subscribe to the theory that inner speech was merely an unvocalized version of social speech, as Piaget claimed. Rather, Vygotsky insisted that, because the functions of inner speech and social speech were different (speech for self versus speech for others), the formal properties of the two types of speech would necessarily be different as well, despite their common social roots (Vygotsky ,1986). Because inner speech is non-vocalized, it is not directly observable. However, Vygotsky argued that the properties of inner speech may be inferred based on the incipient private speech of children as well as the re-emerged private speech of adults (Vygotsky 1986).

Working with young children, Vygotsky found that developing private speech was highly abbreviated. He argued, therefore, that inner speech must be abbreviated in the same way, namely by "omitting the subject of a sentence and all words connected with it, while preserving the predicate" (Vygotsky 1986, p. 236). It must be understood, however, that Vygotsky was referring to "subject" and "predicate" from a functional rather than a grammatical perspective. Thus, his notions of subject and predicate better correspond to the definitions of "psychological subject" and "psychological predicate" (Wertsch, 1979). A psychological subject is what is in a speaker's mind first, the psychological predicate is what is being said about that subject. Given those definitions, the motivation for omitting subjects from inner speech seems transparent. Vygotsky noted that:

> We know what we are thinking about; i.e., we always know the subject and its situation. And since the subject of the inner dialogue is always known, we may just imply it. (1986, p. 242)

A good example of this phenomenon is a simple shopping list, in which people typically write down only the individual items that they wish to buy. They do not tend to write "I must buy soup, I must buy fruit," because the idea "I want to buy" is already known and therefore can be assumed.

Studies of Private Speech and Adult Discourse

By far, most of the research on private speech has focused on children. Nonetheless, adults do use this form of mediation, and although adult private speech may be difficult to observe, it has been the focus of a number of studies, both experimental and naturalistic. The earliest of these studies was that of Soskin and John (1963) which examined the "think aloud" protocols of adults learning new tasks.

Since then, adult speech for the self has been investigated in several settings. They include the "inner writing" found in journals (John-Steiner, 1985a, 1992), the oral production of second language learners, (Ahmed, 1988; Appel, 1986; Brooks & Donato, 1994; Frawley & Lantolf, 1984, 1985; McCafferty, 1992; see McCafferty 1994b for a review of L2 private speech studies), and novice writers in the first language (DiCamilla, 1991; DiCamilla & Lantolf, 1994). The second language studies, beginning with Frawley and Lantolf (1985) have identified several structural and linguistic properties of private speech which distinguish it from social speech. These characteristics do not necessarily constitute a rigid taxonomy, as most researchers would agree that the form of the private speech is dependent on the activity in which it emerges. Indeed Frawley (1992) argues that there must never be such a taxonomy. With that warning in mind, the following characterizations will nonetheless provide a useful frame of reference for discussing private speech and interpreting the data in the following chapters.

Linguistic features of private speech

Frawley and Lantolf (1985) propose a means for categorizing the forms of private speech which appear in discourse, based on the types of regulation (e.g. object-, other-, and self-) that are said to be occurring. Although their system was developed in response to data gained from a picture narration task, the paradigm has been extended to other tasks such as oral reading recall (Appel, 1986; Appel & Lantolf, 1994) and the written production of novice L1 writers (DiCamilla, 1991; DiCamilla & Lantolf, 1994).

Object-regulation corresponds to the most difficult of predicaments: Control is not within an individual's current capacity. One is regulated by the surroundings and only able to respond to what the immediate environment suggests. Drawing from data from a oral picture narration task, Frawley and Lantolf (1985) identify four linguistically based strategies by which the speakers were able to take hold of the task at hand: macrostructure, affective markers, odd pronominalization, and the use of tense and aspect. Subsequent studies have pointed to additional phenomenon: epistemic modality (Ahmed, 1988; DiCamilla, 1991; DiCamilla & Lantolf, 1994), focus (Frawley, 1992) and the use of certain gestures (McCafferty, 1996, 1998; McNeil, 1992).

Macrostructure refers to the presence of extra discursive information as speakers attempt to externalize their inner knowledge of discourse. In the context of a difficult task, externalization is one way of displaying a speaker's knowledge so that it can be manipulated more easily. Thus speakers can get a "grip" on the task and achieve self-regulation by speaking or identifying the task (Frawley & Lantolf, 1985). Speakers impose order on the task by externalizing information about the task at hand, the macrostructure of the task, or even to the speaker's participation in the task (remarks often referred to as "metacomments") as in (1):

> (1) This picture—do want you to tell me, I tell you where he is or? (Frawley & Lantolf, 1985, p. 26)

Additionally, there is an abundance of naming and description, labeling of objects and listing of known information. The preponderance of all this information can cause the discourse to look like "fragmented demonstrations of knowledge" (Frawley & Lantolf, 1985, p. 26). However, the speaker is not intending to relate this knowledge to anyone except herself, in an attempt to control the task and achieve self-regulation.

The use of tense and aspect has also been found to reflect private speech in the discourses of non-native speakers (Ahmed, 1988; Frawley & Lantolf, 1985; Lantolf, DiCamilla, & Ahmed, 1996; McCafferty, 1992, 1994a). Frawley and Lantolf found that in picture narration tasks, intermediate ESL learners often use the past tense, as in (2), while advanced ESL learners and native English speakers preferred instead the atemporal present which is most frequently used in story telling. They argue that the use of the past tense allows the speakers to distance themselves from the events and maintain some control over the task (Frawley & Lantolf, 1985).

> (2) This man, he took the ice cream from the big boy, and the boy became angry because his father took the ice cream and he left. (Frawley & Lantolf, 1985, p. 32)

McCafferty, however, reported that the past tense was used more frequently by advanced learners in coherent discourses than by beginners, who themselves preferred the present progressive tense (McCafferty, 1994a). He suggests that the advanced speakers used the past tense to create coherence by backgrounding certain information. An alternative explanation, however, is that McCafferty's advanced learners, although certainly more proficient that his beginning learners, were still not as advanced as the advanced non-native speakers in Frawley and Lantolf's study who were, for the most part, very proficient graduate students.

In addition to the strategic deployment of the past tense, Frawley and Lantolf (1985) discovered that speakers who were almost entirely object-regulated in respect to the picture narration task used the present progressive. The use of the progressive causes the narration to be presented as a series of separate and unrelated events, as in describing photos (e.g. "here we are sitting on the beach, there we are feeding the dolphins..."). Such "narrations" are reminiscent of the fragmented demonstrations of knowledge brought about by the deluge of externalized information associated with naming and labeling.

The continued pronominalization of thematic characters throughout the discourse despite shifts in reference is characteristic of the picture narration discourse, as seen in (3).

(3) A little boy is went out in [...] went out for a walk. He met the ice cream man and he got an ice cream cone and he [...] gave the ice cream cone to the little boy and he drank it all. (Frawley & Lantolf, 1985, p. 37)

To the outsider, the narration may seem chaotic or confusing, because it is not clear to whom the speaker, an L1 child, is referring. It seems unlikely that the speaker is being purposely unclear in order to confuse the experimenter. Instead, the speaker is engaging in private speech, which, as will be recalled, is predicative and abbreviated in nature. In that case, the speaker addresses no one but herself, and thus pronominalization is not a problem, because she always knows to whom she is referring.

Focus is a strategy of private speech first discussed by Frawley (1992) in an L1 (cross-linguistic) study of linguistic mediation that appears to complement the ambiguous reference described above. Frawley showed that, when faced with a cognitive problem, speakers often retain forms which otherwise might have been abbreviated, according to the particular strategies that a given language permits in order to avoid redundancy (such as pronominalization, null pronouns, coordination, and ellipsis). Thus, as opposed to ambiguous, the resulting discourse appears redundant. Frawley argues that this phenomenon occurs when, for whatever reason, the topic is the object of the speaker's ongoing mental activity. The retained forms allow the speaker to externalize and potentially to resolve the problem at hand.

Metacomments and epistemic modality are means by which speakers express their attitudes about the truth value of their own utterances, presumably because they are not in control of the information (DiCamilla & Lantolf, 1994; McCafferty, 1994a). Utterances containing only relevant information are presented as truth, while statements prefaced by "I think" or "it seems" indicate that the speaker is operating at the level of belief (DiCamilla & Lantolf, 1994), as in (4):

(4) He's walking the street. I think that the boy is trying to buy ice cream. (Frawley & Lantolf, 1985, p. 32)

Additionally, the use of modal verbs such as "should" and "must" suggests that the speaker has merely induced or deduced the information being presented, and is unwilling to commit to the truth value of the utterance.

In other-regulation, control is in the hands of another, more capable person. Private speech connected with other- regulation may be an attempt to give the control to the other so that the task may be completed successfully. This may be realized via questions to the experimenter or to the self, as a sort of surrogate other (McCafferty, 1994a) (5):

(5) This is, I think, the rule. What do you call it? (Frawley & Lantolf, 1985, p. 30)

Self-regulation is achieved after object- and other-regulation is overcome. It is the state being of able to control the self and the task. Private speech associated with self-regulation consists of those metacomments that indicate that the individual has suddenly understood or resolved a difficulty in the task, as in (6).

(6) Oh, now I see. (McCafferty 1992, p. 184)

Most of the examples presented here to illustrate the linguistic properties of private speech have been taken from non-native discourse. However, it is important to bear in mind that the presence of private speech it not an exclusive feature of second language production. Private speech can and does occur in the discourses of adult native speakers when the task at hand represents cognitive difficulty for the individual and as long the individual is not inhibited (John-Steiner, 1992). A number of studies, beginning with Soskin & John (1963), have found evidence of private speech in the L1 adult discourse. Frawley and Lantolf (1985) and Ahmed (1988) looked at both native and non-native speakers, and found consistent evidence of private speech in the speech of the natives, albeit to a lesser degree than that of the non-natives on the same task. Appel (1986), comparing native and non-native recall protocols, found that the native English speakers actually produced more private speech than their L2 counterparts. This finding she attributes to cultural and social differences between the two groups, a conclusion that is further supported by McCafferty's (1994b) cross-cultural study of private speech. The presence of peculiar forms even in native discourse allows us to argue that not all errors found in non-native discourse are the result of low proficiency (Frawley & Lantolf 1984, 1985).

Private writing
DiCamilla and Lantolf's (1994) analysis of novice writers and the linguistic properties of private speech is especially relevant to the present study for several reasons: one, because they find evidence of private speech in written production, and two, because the language of the production is the writers' native language. Specifically, DiCamilla and Lantolf, like John-Steiner (1985a, 1992), argue that the externalization of inner speech is not limited to oral speech. Instead, inner speech can be externalized in writing. When faced with a cognitively difficult task, writers deploy certain linguistic devices that create cognitive distance and help orient or reorient their attention in order to be self-regulated in their writing activity (DiCamilla & Lantolf 1994, p. 365).

The written externalization of inner speech is referred to as private writing and serves the same cognitive function as private speech, namely maintaining vigilance and control over higher mental functions (DiCamilla & Lantolf, 1994). Furthermore, as DiCamilla and Lantolf found, private writing exhibits many of the same linguistic features as private speech. Thus, the use of what appear to be odd forms of deixis, anaphors, modality, tense, and aspect in writing can be interpreted as the writers' attempts to gain control of a difficult task such as, in the case of that study, learning how to produce coherent and cohesive written texts in their native language.

Again, that these communicatively odd forms occur in the native language as well as the L2, supports Frawley and Lantolf's (1985) original argument that these forms do not necessarily reflect the speaker's underlying competence. After all, it is not reasonable to suggest that native speakers do not possess native competence. A more convincing explanation is that the speech, while seemingly odd, is instead speech for the self, with the purpose of attaining or regaining control in an activity.

EXPERIMENTAL METHODOLOGY IN SOCIOCULTURAL RESEARCH

As has been noted before, Vygotsky was critical of the research of the behaviorist and mentalist psychologies of his day, because they conflated the object of study with the explanatory principle. He denounced the experimental methods of these frameworks as well. Vygotsky argued that reaction time experiments and introspection, their respective experimental paradigms, were inadequate measures of complex psychological processes and activities (Vygotsky, 1978). In the same way, he dismissed methods borrowed from the natural sciences that treated learners as inert objects instead of unique agents (Lantolf & Appel, 1994). This section presents Vygotsky's own methodological framework, his Genetic Method and discusses the purpose and procedures behind the present study.

Vygotsky's Genetic Method

Vygotsky's rejection of behaviorist and mentalist paradigms stems, no doubt, from his ideas about the complexity of activity and the role of individuals in determining the nature of activity. It is also the case that, because of his focus on activity, his experimental goals were different than those working in other paradigms. Instead of mere description, Vygotsky sought an explanation of mental behavior. At the same time, he rejected any attempt to predict mental activity (Lantolf & Appel, 1994). Given the complex and individual nature of human activity, it is clear Vygotsky thought that, with regard to psychological behavior, prediction is impossible.

Vygotsky argued that higher mental functions could only be understood as processes rather than products, and that these processes could only be studied socially and genetically (developmentally). As an alternative to the research methods of the other paradigms, he proposed the "Genetic Method" (Vygotsky, 1978), an approach which focused on the emergence and development of psychological processes across four genetic domains: phylogenetic, sociocultural (or historical), ontogenetic, and microgenetic.

The notion of mediation is central to the explanatory principles of each genetic domain (Wertsch, 1985b). The phylogenetic domain deals with the biological evolution of higher mental functions in humans as a species. Vygotsky saw this domain as primarily concerned with the organic development necessary for humans to use physical and psychological tools. The sociocultural domain deals with the social and cultural conditions out of which tool use arises. The ontogenetic domain is concerned with the emergence of mediational means in child development and must take into account the intertwining of biological and social influences. The microgenetic domain involves a dual set of explanatory principles (biological and social) and is concerned with the short term formation of psychological processes (Wertsch, 1985b).

Most of Vygotsky's own research was concerned with ontogenesis. In the experimental setting (microgenesis), researchers investigate psychological processes genetically by forcing their emergence. One way to accomplish this is to confront the person with a difficulty or with disruptions in the flow of the task (Lantolf & Appel, 1994). This allows the researcher to observe how changes (i.e. development) occur as a result of the interference. This is especially true of research that attempts to investigate the mediational role of language. For this reason, the present study employs a task that is assumed to be sufficiently difficult for the learners as to require them to mediate their meaning-making processes externally through their written linguistic activity, and thus allow these processes to be at least in part observable.

Purpose of the Study

This study is an investigation of the meaning-making activity of text comprehension and recall as realized by L2 learners and as mediated by language, through an analysis of the written recall protocols produced following the reading of a first or second language text. Based on the constructivist view of text comprehension elaborated in Chapter 1, the production of a recall text is understood to consist of the recreating or possibly even the creating of meaning based on, but not limited to, the target texts. The activity of meaning-reconstruction at the time of writing would imply that the reader was initially able to construct a reasonable amount of meaning at the time of reading. Thus, there ought to be linguistic features that suggest that the learners were engaged in the socially oriented activity of relating known or familiar information in the protocols. However, because the experimental texts themselves are of some length and difficulty, it is understood that the actual writing of the protocols may tend toward the privately (or problem solving) oriented mental activity of comprehending the text. That is, the learners may create meaning during the recall instead of simply reconstructing meaning that was initially shaped at the time of reading. Thus, the language of the protocols is expected at times to reflect the on-going mental process of comprehension or meaning-construction, that is, problem-solving activity, externalized in, and mediated by writing.

Following Vygostky's claim that higher psychological processes are mediated by language, the study seeks to explore the processes involved in reading comprehension and recall as they are linguistically mediated. Therefore, the study investigates language as it represents the externalized activity of the mind in the face of cognitive difficulty. Human activity, as it has been argued, is context-dependent and dynamic, and, therefore, likely to differ between and within individuals as it unfolds. Thus, the study additionally seeks to discover ways in which the language that mediates an individual's activity can inform us about the individual's activity, in this case, that of ostensibly producing a recall protocol. In particular, we hope to find out something about the learners' orientation to the activity in which they are engaged.

The learners' activity and, particularly, the mediational properties of their task-generated language will be explored by examining the linguistic features of their recall protocols. Previous work on private speech provides a starting point for the present analysis, and the protocols will be examined for signs of some of the more prototypical characteristics of private speech (e.g. odd tense, aspect, modality). Because this study involves a combination of tasks not previously employed in the framework of Sociocultural Theory, however, it is likely, given the complexity and uniqueness of human activity, that different forms or new functions of known forms of private speech may be revealed. Thus, in this exploration of the mediational properties of language, it is essential not to interpret previous findings as constituting a strict taxonomy of private speech features.

Because the recall protocols are written, the linguistic features of the protocols will be discussed in terms of private writing. Signs of private writing in the recalls will be interpreted as evidence that the learners have had difficulty achieving and maintaining self-regulation in the task. Crucially, in this task, the difficulty should not lie in the language of the recall, since it is the learners' native language. Rather we expect the difficulties to lie in the different texts, in some cases because of the formal local properties, that is, the language of the text, and in others because of the content.

As mentioned above, this study additionally seeks to discover what private writing can tell us about the activity in which the learners are engaged, particularly at the level of orientation. That is, the way in which the learners view or approach the task in light of the potential difficulties that the task might present. Task-based research, including reading research, assumes that the learners approach experimental tasks with the orientation prescribed by the researcher and, crucially, maintain that orientation throughout the duration of the task. Because private writing represents the external semiotic mediation of the learners' mental activity, a careful analysis of its features may offer evidence as to their orientation at the outset of the task as well as to any shifts in orientation and changes in activity which may occur as they attempt to establish and maintain focus in the task.

Participants

Thirty-two students of Spanish as a second language at Cornell University participated in the study. Twenty-seven of the learners were enrolled in one of three sections of a third semester, elementary level Spanish course as the result of their performance on a standardized placement exam. The remaining five learners were enrolled in an intermediate level class, and were essentially two semesters ahead of the elementary learners. All were native speakers of English, five were bilingual speakers of English and of another home or second language (Hindi, Jamaican Patois, Japanese, Hebrew, Russian).

Learners from different class levels were used to bring out differences in performance as a result of the difficulty of the task, as relative to the learners' second language proficiency. The 27 elementary level learners were invited to participate in the experiment during class time and, although they were given the opportunity to refuse, all students present in class chose to participate. The five intermediate learners were self-selected and had come to participate in the experiment after responding to a general announcement made in their Spanish class. Some researchers, especially those working in a quantitatively oriented paradigm might object to the 27:5 ratio of elementary to intermediate learners, arguing that statistical comparison between the groups may be impossible because a sample size of five is unlikely to be representative of the population. While that may be the case, it is important to keep in mind that the lack of advanced learners does not affect this study in the same way, because of its emphasis on individual agents and complex activity from a hermeneutic perspective. Any research in the framework of activity by definition rejects the notion of representative samples, and would not, in fact, expect there to be discrete, categorical differences between populations.[14]

Procedures

The administration of the study involved a set of instructions and three experimental texts (see Appendix B for a copy of the task instructions, and Appendix C for copies of the experimental texts).[15] Given the decision to explore the linguistic mediation of mind as externalized in the face of a problem, the experimental texts were chosen to represent differing degrees of difficulty, as a result of either the text language or the content. The experimental texts included a newspaper report in Spanish, a newspaper report in English, and an expository text in English. Both the newspaper texts were authentic articles that dealt with political issues in Latin America, of which it was hoped that the students would have no more than vague or general knowledge. The English newspaper text was modified for length. The expository text, taken from an encyclopedia entry, was about physics, and was considered to be difficult because of its content.

These texts were chosen in order to allow for comparison of reading across and within languages. The expectancy was that the L2 newspaper text, by virtue of being in Spanish, would be more difficult to comprehend than the L1 newspaper text. At the same time, the L1 expository text was expected to be more difficult than the L1 newspaper article, by virtue of the former's content and the assumed familiarity with newspaper texts on the part of the learners. Thus, the relative difficulty of the three texts can be expressed in following equation (7):

(7) L2 newspaper $\geq$ L1 expository $>$ L1 newspaper

The L2 newspaper text is of equal or higher difficulty than the L1 expository text and both are more difficult than the L1 newspaper text, but for different reasons (i.e. the language versus the content of the texts). The difference in difficulty is expected to be reflected in the language of the recall protocols, as the learners worked at gaining and maintaining regulation in the activity of producing a recall text.

The three sections of elementary learners participated in the experiment during their regular class period. Two of the classes were the researcher's own sections, while the third was taught by another instructor who was present during, and assisted in, the administering of the experiment. Two of the intermediate learners participated in the experiment along with one of the three intermediate classes, and the other three were administered the task individually during an appointment with the researcher.

The learners were first given a sheet with instructions and allowed several minutes to read through and to ask questions. Each text was then administered separately. The learners were given four minutes to read each text, after which they were required to turn the page over, and to write on a second sheet of paper in English as much as they could remember of what they had read. They were allotted six minutes for writing the protocol. There was a short break of approximately four minutes between the administering of the texts. To avoid any practice effects, the texts were administered in the order of most to least difficult (as shown in (7) above). In that way, any improvement due to practice would only affect the easier texts.

Given our earlier discussion of task, it is appropriate to point out here that the materials and the procedures described above constitute a task, that is, an activity blueprint. A single task, as has been argued, can generate a multitude of activities on the part of the learners. This task reflects, of course, the researcher's orientation to the study and desire to set certain parameters on the activity of the learners in the midst of this variability. However, often times, and as was the case in this study, activity varies along lines not entirely predicted by the researcher. The specific nature of that variation will be the focus of the discussion in the following chapters.

SUMMARY

In this chapter, I have argued that consciousness is neither a purely subjective nor a purely reflective phenomena, nor is it an abstract representation of processes which underlie mental activity. Instead, consciousness is mental activity, organized dynamically and symbolically, constructed through discourse, and observable in activity.

Mental activity arises out of meaningful human interaction and meaning-making. Thus, the context of activity is the appropriate setting for an investigation of consciousness. Activity, like consciousness, is itself a complex and dynamic phenomenon not reducible to its component parts. The complex and dynamic nature of activity, as it is carried out by real human individuals who are themselves shaped by their own discourses, leads to the inevitable, although not tragic, result that activity is always realized differently and not predictable beforehand.

Self-regulation is one example of mental activity that perhaps deserves a special status among the higher mental functions, since it is potentially involved in the execution of all other behavior. Like other mental activities, regulation is mediated by language—inner and private speech. Research in the Vygotskian tradition has investigated the linguistic forms of private speech, thus identifying, for certain contexts, some of its formal properties. Analyzing the presence of private speech in discourse helps the researcher to determine the status of the individual with regard to regulation. Embedded, as always, in the context of an activity, an analysis of private speech can shed light on the activity in which the individual is attempting regulation.

The purpose of this study, then, is to discover more about reading and reconstructing native and non-native language texts, through an analysis of the language generated by the learners' activity in the task presented to them. By adhering to Vygotsky's Genetic Method and presenting the learners with readings of some difficulty, and by taking previous studies on private speech and writing as reference point, we hope to find out more about the processes involved in text comprehension and recall. Because we are dealing with unique individuals whose motives and intentions are necessarily different, we expect that the task of reading and recalling L1 and L2 texts will result in the realization of different types of activity.

NOTES

[1]   For the purpose of this discussion, no theoretical distinction will be made between mind and consciousness.

[2]   It should be pointed out that by consciousness Vygotsky did not mean simply awareness, but rather, mental functioning, and particularly, the ability to regulate oneself while solving complex problems (Lantolf & Appel, 1994, p. 3).

[3]   It is important to make note of the distinction that will be made between mental activity and activity. Mental activity is used to refer to the dynamic mental functioning that comprises consciousness. Activity, for the most part, refers to specific human behavior, or the functioning of humans, both psychological and physical, as this occurs in socioculturally defined contexts.

[4]   Vygotsky distinguished between lower mental functions (including input systems such as vision, hearing, tactile and olfactory systems, as well as natural memory and involuntary attention) and higher mental functions (including logical memory, planning, perception, problem solving, and voluntary attention). Lower, or natural, mental functions, are shared with animals. Higher, or cultural, mental functions, however, crucially evolve out of lower functions as the result of symbolic mediation in a unique sociocultural milieu, arising from "the interweaving of thought and speech" (Frawley, 1987, p.142). Higher functions are characterized by voluntary control, social origins and conscious mediation by psychological tools (Wertsch, 1985b).

[5]   It is at this point where the ideas of Vygotsky's successors begin to diverge markedly from those of Vygotsky himself. It was proposed by A. N. Leontiev and the Kharkovites that activity could be both the explanatory principle and the unit of analysis. The theoretical validity of this position continues to be a source of great controversy in the field. Although the present discussion will avoid this debate, the reader is referred to Kozulin (1986, 1990) for a detailed exposition of the history of Activity Theory.

[6]   For example, the advent of electronic mail, at the very least, has changed the way in which some people engage in written, personal communication.

[7]   Genetic explanation will be taken up later in this chapter.

[8]   For a discussion of the acquisition of mediational means, the reader is referred to Vygotsky (1978).

[9]   It is not necessary to go into the sociohistorical conditions which brought this particular activity into existence. However, it should be obvious to those familiar with the game that it is a product of a specific sociohistorical setting which sanctions both capitalistic activity and play, outside of which this activity may not be determined to be appropriate. For example, it is hard to imagine a hunting or gathering society having an interest in Monopoly™.

[10]   These may, in fact, also be analyzed as the goals of the activity "leisure time," another example of a socioculturally determined activity.

[11]   A. A. Leontiev (1991) argued that this distinction is not unimportant, as the "shape" of the tool (in this case, language) crucially alters the process.

[12]   This is intended to be a representative rather than an exhaustive list of possible activities for this task.

[13]   Vygotsky himself used the Piagetian term "egocentric speech." Flavell (1966) suggested the use of "private speech," the most widely accepted term, which will be used throughout subsequent discussion.

[14]   See, for example, Appel (1986), who using a quantitative analysis of hesitation patterns and a qualitative analysis of private speech features and other factors, found no categorical differences between native and non-native readers of English.

[15]   The experimental texts are labeled as follows: the Spanish newspaper article = Text A, the English newspaper article = Text B, the English expository text = Text C. This labeling does not reflect the order in which the experimental texts were administered, but, for ease of exposition, correspond to the order in which the texts are discussed in the following chapters, as well as the order in which they are presented in Appendix C.

3

The L2 Protocols[1]

This chapter presents an analysis of the linguistic features of the recall protocols of the sole L2 text, a newspaper article in Spanish. As will be seen in the ensuing discussion, the recalls present abundant evidence of language which can only be characterized as private writing in that it is reflective of the problem-solving activity of the learners. Particularly, the language of the protocols reveals the difficulties encountered as learners attempted to complete the task of comprehending the target text and producing a recall protocol. The writing at times betrays the learners' lack of control and, in some cases, is indicative of various strategies that the learners employed in an attempt to gain and maintain control during the task.

That the learners find the task difficult should come as no surprise, given the time limit imposed on the reading of the text and the writing of the recall, as well as the difficulty of the text relative to the learners' level of L2 proficiency. While the following analysis deals with the linguistic properties of the recall protocols, and not with the propositional content, even a cursory analysis of such content would reveal the challenge that this text posed to the students. The amount of extra-textual information present in the recall protocols, for example, suggests that learners were forced to rely heavily on world knowledge in order to compensate for the limited amount of meaning they were able to create based on the text alone. Additionally, the inaccuracies in the protocols reveal that most learners had only limited access to the syntactic and lexical information in the text.

The protocols were filled with some of the better-described instances of private speech. This provided further evidence that the reading and recalling of this particular text was sufficiently difficult to cause, in some cases, the learners to mediate their comprehension of the text externally in their attempt to the complete the task. The following analysis, then, presents and discusses the different private speech features evident in the protocols, with the ultimate goal of determining properties of the learners' activity in the task of reading and recall.

MACROSTRUCTURE

Macrostructure is a feature of private speech described by Frawley and Lantolf (1985) as consisting of the way in which learners externalize their knowledge of discourse and their metalinguistic organization of the discourse, often times at the commencement of a task, in an attempt to "grab hold" of the task. In the sociocultural literature, the term macrostructure has been defined in several different, although not unrelated, ways. Frawley and Lantolf use macrostructure in a broad sense to refer to different sorts of knowledge that a speaker may externalize regarding a certain discourse, including knowledge about its organization, structure, topic, and even characters, as they found to be the case for their picture narration task.

Appel & Lantolf (1994) use macrostructure in a more restricted sense, borrowing from van Dijk & Kintsch's (1983) work on text comprehension to refer only to the global semantic meaning assigned to a text by a speaker or reader during comprehension. This definition of macrostructure corresponds to the notion of "theme, gist, upshot, point" (van Dijk & Kintsch, 1983, p. 189). For van Dijk and Kintsch the typical summary macrostructure is best described by the formula "X is about Y" where the first half of the formula (X) serves to label the discourse in question and the second (Y) attempts to assign it a global meaning (van Dijk & Kintsch, 1983, p. 191). In short, macrostructures are summary statements constructed out of the macropropositions contained in the discourse. Summary macrostructures are crucial to the comprehension of lengthy texts, and van Dijk and Kintsch have found that people develop them during reading, regardless of whether they were asked to do so or not, and whether or not the macrostructures were explicitly expressed in the text (van Dijk & Kintsch, 1983, p. 233).

The relevant aspect of macrostructure is not so much whether one is referring to knowledge about the structure or the content of a text, but rather the fact that in difficult situations, speakers and writers initially tend to externalize this information. Thus, discourses are labeled, named, described as well as summarized at the outset of production in an attempt to get hold of the information to be related. These strategies, according to Frawley and Lantolf (1985), ought to be interpreted as attempts to gain control of, and thus begin, the task. They are strategies for knowing the discourse, with the ultimate goal of relating the discourse.

In writing the Spanish newspaper recall protocols, learners expressed both descriptive and summary information at the outset of the task. This is perhaps not surprising, since newspaper texts in particular present powerful cues for the generation of such macrostructures, including captions, headlines and datelines (van Dijk & Kintsch ,1983, p. 209). Additionally, newspaper reports are often structured such that a summary sentence or paragraph appears in initial position. Some of the labeling and naming found in the protocols can be seen in the following examples (1-6) (see Appendix A for a list of the symbols used in the typed transcription of the recalls).[2]

(1)   Article written 10/28/92 [101A]
(2)   Regarding the "Torricelli Bill" [124A]
(3)   Oct. 28 - Miami [115A]
(4)   Miami; United States Oct . 28. [119A]
(5)   Miami United States of America 28th [106A]
(6)   28 octubre [122A]

Examples (1) and (2) present fairly straightforward examples of macrostructures in the form of a label. In (1), the learner made overt reference to and labeled one aspect of the task, namely the text itself. In (2), the learner appears to have titled the forthcoming recall by recollecting the topic of the text. This heading is a somewhat awkward way of beginning a recall directed at a reader, in the sense that it presupposes that the reader of the protocols already knows something about the "Torricelli law." This is probably an indication that the writing is not oriented toward the reader, but rather toward the writer, who by externalizing some aspect of the text at the outset, attempts to get hold of the information he is going to recall.

Examples (3-6) resemble the dateline which typically precedes a newspaper article, and which, in fact, preceded this experimental text. The production of a newspaper looking recall protocol is thus an interesting but not unusual orientation to the task of recalling a newspaper text. One might argue, especially in the case of (3-4), that learners had not labeled the task in an attempt to gain control, rather, they were merely oriented toward replicating the original text verbatim. Nevertheless, we cannot rule out the possibility that the production of a macrostructure somehow facilitated the recall process, by allowing learners to begin the task by recalling relatively brief and perhaps salient information.

Looking at examples (5-6), it is clear that for several learners control was a problem at the time of producing the macrostructures. In effect, the manner in which these macrostructures were developed may inform us about the learners' state of control. For example, in (5), the learner externalized more information, namely, the spelling out of the "United States of America," than what was present in the dateline of original text (*EEUU* "USA"). One reasonable explanation is that the writer had developed a lengthy (and arguably redundant) macrostructure in order to gain time and achieve temporal and cognitive distance, and thus obtain control in the task. Thus, the spell-out of the entire phrase may be the written equivalent of an unfilled pause which speakers often make use of in order to form their thoughts.

That this learner had been writing for his own benefit—that is, with the purpose of knowing the information as opposed to relating it—is especially evident in his mention of the date using the day (28th) but not the month.[3] As will be discussed in detail further below, information which is presumably known to the writer but not made explicit for the reader is characteristic of private speech in that it indicates that the writer is engaged in problem-solving as opposed to a communicative activity.[4] Thus, the evidence points to this learner as having encountered some difficulty in beginning the task, and having externalized extra-discursive information about the text as a way in which to secure control in the task.

The learner in (6) also appears to have had some difficulty with the task. In this particular case, she was apparently dominated by the language of the original text, which she was forced to use as the language of the recall, at least temporarily. It is interesting to note that while the initial mention of the date is in the language of the original text (Spanish), the learner then wrote "On Oct. 28, George Bush," thus reconstructing the date in English. By externalizing some information about the task, albeit in Spanish, the learner was able to gain control over the information and present it in the appropriate language and, furthermore, as an integrated part of the recall protocol.

As with any other task, the learners in this experiment needed to commence the task of producing a recall protocol in one way or another. People engaged in task-based activity often begin to do so by developing a plan of action, based on their initial orientation to and assessment of the task. With regard to speech production, Appel & Lantolf (1994) have discovered that one thing that people do when faced with cognitively difficult situations is to externalize the planning process by speaking. That is, people formulate their plan for speaking by speaking to themselves. Furthermore, Appel & Lantolf have determined, with respect to text comprehension and recall, that one way of planning the discourse is through the externalization of a summary of the text.

It is important to point out that the Spanish newspaper text, like most newspaper articles, begins with an abstract component that establishes the main point of the article by presenting a summary of the principle event of the report. An abstract component differs somewhat from van Dijk & Kintsch's (1983) description of a typical summary macrostructure, in that it lacks the initial labeling component (i.e. most newspaper articles do not begin with "this is a story about"). Nonetheless, the abstract (called the lead in newspaper terminology) provides a summary of the article, and is one of the principal characteristics which distinguishes newspaper articles from another, more common type of narrative, the personal narrative, which is less likely to begin this way (Bell, 1991).

Given the organization of the original text, it is hardly surprising that some learners began their protocols with a similar sort of summarizing statement, as in the following examples (7-11):

(7)   On the 28th of October in Miami Florida, George Bush signed a law that prohib-
       its American owned businesses in other countries from trading with Fidel Cas-
       tros [sic] Cuba. [112A]
(8)   Pres. Bush signed a controversial act for Cuban Democracy. [202A]
(9)   On the 28 of October George Bush, in Miami, signed a law concerning Cuba.
       [105A]
(10)   October 28 Bush signs law - the Torricelli law. [108 A]
(11)   Bush declares that he will not rest "until all of the Cubans are all free." [113A]

The above excerpts, with the exception of (11), are alike in the sense that they cap-
ture some of the information presented in the lead of the original newspaper text.
The initial summaries, no doubt related to the structure of the original text, may
have facilitated the learners' recall by providing them with an organizing strategy.
   The relative complexity of the summaries in (7-10) allows us to say something
about the learners' mental activity and orientation at the time of writing. For
example, it seems logical to assume that writers who present more detailed and
clearer language (7-8) were in greater control of the linguistic resources of the
text than others whose abstracts were either vague (9) or brief (10). What is particularly interesting about (10) is the modification, or rather, clarification, which
follows the dash. This learner had constructed a rather short summary of the article ("Bush signs law") which she was then able to expand on in the same line by
adding more detail. Thus, by externalizing what she knew about the text, she was
able to generate further information. The opening line in (11) refers back to one
of the last lines of the original text, suggesting that the learner had not intended
to write a summary of the article, rather she was simply remembering which she
had read last.
   The protocols contained several examples of summary macrostructures. What is
curious about macrostructures of this type is that they contain a label, which,
unlike the abstract, is not directly suggested by or mentioned in the original article
(van Dijk & Kintsch, 1983). In this way, the summary macrostructure, through its
labeling component, may serve the cognitive function of naming the task and
through its abstract component, may be a plan or knowing strategy for the subsequent discourse. Examples of summary macrostructures can be seen in (12-14):

(12)   This is a news article [...] about the Oct 23rd signing of the Torricelli law act by
       George Bush. [204A]
(13)   This is about George Bush, the president of the United States on Friday the 23rd,
       talking about the policy towards Cubans. [118A]
(14)   This little writing thing delt [sic] with the relations between the United States,
       and its allies (France, Britain, Canada etc.) and Cuba. [127A]

The learners appear to have begun the recall similarly, yet the macrostructures
reveal significant differences among individual learners with respect to their control of the task. The writer in (12) unequivocally stated that she was writing about

a news article and gave a brief summary, thus demonstrating a fair amount of control as she began the task. However, in contrast, the macrostructure presented in (13), reveals that the writer was neither entirely in control of the task nor even of the writing of the macrostructure. For example, the writer failed to completely identify the text that she was recalling, referring instead to "this." As was seen with (5) earlier, and as will be discussed in more detail below, the use of what to a reader appears to be ambiguous language and, particularly, pronominal reference, suggests that the language itself is directed at the writer (for whom "this" is not ambiguous). In the same way, the lack of precision in referring to the text in (14) indicates that the writer also encountered difficulty establishing control.

An externalized macrostructure was also evident when learners attempted to produce a recall protocol which approximated the discursive structure (what van Dijk & Kintsch, 1983, refer to as the "superstructure") of a particular genre. In most cases, this was a newspaper-like opening. As seen in previous examples, this often involved the reproduction of several of the discursive features of the newspaper article, namely the presence of a title and a dateline. Again, replicating the discursive structure of the original text in itself may not be an unusual choice in light of the task. However, there were two instances in which the discursive structure produced in the recall protocols was not suggested by the task nor the text. In these cases, the learners began the recalls in almost a story-like manner (15-16):

(15)   It is October 23 in Miami, Florida and President Bush has formulated a law that directly affects the Cuban American community. [111A]
(16)   It was the 28th, of October, a Friday. [125A]

Newspaper articles are clearly stories, both in the sense that they are referred to as such (i.e. Did you read that story in yesterday's paper about Bob Feller?) and also because they exhibit features common to stories (e.g. characters, abstract, orientation, action) (Bell, 1981). Nonetheless, newspaper stories differ sharply from other types of narratives because they obligatorily begin with an abstract component, followed by an orientation section, which provides background information about the events and characters introduced in the abstract. Personal narratives, for example, usually omit the abstract component, beginning instead with the orientation or background segment, often introduced by formulaic utterances, such as "it was" or "once upon a time."

The opening lines in (15) and (16) suggest that some learners treated the newspaper discourse, at least initially, as a personal narrative, by skipping the often missing abstract component and beginning with an orientation segment. One possible explanation is that these learners, encountering difficulty at the outset of the task, needed to employ an arguably more familiar genre in order to achieve self-regulation in the task of relating information about a newspaper text. Appel and Lantolf (1994) found similar results, namely, a learner who explicitly referred to an expository text about the care of coffee plants as a story.

TENSE AND ASPECT

As discussed in Chapter 2, particular uses of tense and aspect have been found to be indicative of private speech in the discourses of native and non-native speakers (Ahmed, 1988; DiCamilla & Lantolf, 1994; Frawley & Lantolf, 1984, 1985; McCafferty, 1992, 1994a). Namely, it has been shown that for oral story telling tasks, the use of the present and the present progressive indicates an inability to distance oneself from the events of the text, the use of the past suggests strategic distancing, and the atemporal present is indicative of control of the narrative (Ahmed, 1988; Frawley & Lantolf, 1985). The deployment of tense and aspect in the recall protocols in this study, however, can only be assessed by first considering the tenses in the original text.

As would be expected for a newspaper piece of this kind, the Spanish text report employed past tense for most of the article to describe completed actions, and some present and future tenses to describe continuing states. A learner who was able to maintain control ought to show a pattern of tenses similar to that in the original text. Such is the case in the protocol presented below (17a-f):

(17)   a.   In an attempt to forward his campaign, President George Bush <u>signed</u> the "Torricelli" law on the 23rd of October.
       b.   In signing the bill, Bush <u>hoped</u> to raise his popularity ^with (and gain the support of) the Hispanic Americans in Florida.
       c.   Sen. Torricelli <u>was</u> in attendance, along w/ the Senator of Florida.
       d.   The bill itself <u>guarantees</u> $247, 000 of the National Defense Budget to third world countries in an attempt to stop Cuban leader Fidel Castro ^**from taking them over.**
       e.   Bush <u>vowed</u> that "Castro should/must fall."
       f.   Bush also <u>made</u> it a point to say that he <u>hopes</u> that someday all countries <u>will be</u> democratically run. [126A]

Much like what is found in the original text, this learner employed the past tense for the past events and states (17a) "signed," (17b) "hoped," (17c) "was," (17f) "made," and the present and future tenses for present and future actions (17d) "guarantees," (17f) "hopes." This use is appropriate in that it is coherent and consistent with the original text.[5]

The use of the atemporal present and the progressive are indicative of object-regulation, in that control is situated in the text and not in the learner. The deployment of the atemporal present is essentially linked to the learner's treatment of the text as a narrative, that is, a story. It has been proposed that the orientation toward producing a text of a more familiar and thus more manageable genre is a response to the difficulties encountered in the task. The present progressive reflects an even lesser degree of control, suggesting that the learner was overwhelmed with the immediacy of the events in the text and was unable to sort them out or tie them together (Ahmed, 1988; Frawley & Lantolf, 1985).[6] Both tenses are found in the following excerpt (18a-i):

(18)   a.   Oct 28 Bush <u>signs</u> law?The Torricelli law.
       b.   Senator Bob Graham and Torricelli both <u>are</u> supporters of the law.
       c.   The law <u>is</u> for the democracy of Cuba.
       d.   Bush <u>is visiting</u> Miami on his electoral campaign.
       e.   Bush <u>gives</u> a speech [...] about how the U.S. <u>will</u> continue to fight the regime of Castro.
       f.   <u>will</u> continue to work against the Communists [sic] of Cuba
       g.   so that the Miamians <u>will</u> once again be united with their families in their homeland.
       h.   Bush <u>is</u> against the Communists of Cuba
       i.   and the US <u>has in the past pursued</u> [end of protocol] [108A]

This recall is particularly revealing because of the different tenses employed and the way in which the learner alternates between them. This variation illustrates how control, and thus orientation, fluctuated, as the learner proceeded through the recall task. For most of the recall, this learner alternated between advancing the narration with the atemporal present (18a, e) and being caught by the immediacy of the events and states, as evidenced by the present progressive (18d) and present tense (18b, c, h). This alternation reflects differing degrees of control. At times, the learner was sufficiently in control such that she was able to relate the information as part of a cohesive text, albeit a narrative. At others, we find that the control of task lay firmly in the text, which overwhelmed the learner with its immediacy. Thus, the writer, much like the object-regulated child, was reduced to describing the facts of the text (Frawley & Lantolf, 1985).

At the end of the recall, however, the learner switched to the appropriate past tense. The shift in orientation and control is reflected in the content of the recall at this point, for it is here that the learner began to discuss extra-textual knowledge (18i). Because it comes from her own world-knowledge about U.S.-Cuban relations, this is information that she is presumably more certain of and able to relate via an appropriate tense. What remains unknown is why the learner chose to relate extra-textual information. Perhaps, she was unaware that she was doing so, or maybe it was a conscious, strategic choice to finish the recall in this way. In any case, the appropriate present perfect tense indicates that at this point control of the information was not a problem.

Most learners used both appropriate and inappropriate tenses in their recalls, again, suggesting that the struggle for self-regulation was arduous, yet characterized by brief moments of success (19a-k).

(19)   a.   Bush <u>declares</u> that he will not rest until all of the Cubans are free.
       b.   He also <u>says</u> that Castro must fall.
       c.   600 hundred ^**Cuban** cities <u>agree</u> with him.

   d. $247,000 <u>was put</u> into this
   e.   Trade <u>is affected</u>.
   f.   ^A Representative from New Jersey and a senator <u>were</u> there, uninvited.
   g.   Bush <u>is</u> <u>doing</u> all he can to bring about the fall of Fidel Castro.
   h.   There <u>were</u> petitions and
   i.   France and Canada <u>were</u> involved.
   j.   They <u>are going</u> to block off trade.
   k.   and <u>support</u> the people of Cuba to bring his rain [sic] down and [end] [113A]

Here the learner alternated between the present and the past.[7] Interestingly, she used the past tenses in those propositions which carry only general information, such as in lines (19h) and (19i). The restricted use of the past tense is evidence that the learner was in control of the general information in the text. That is, she was able to identify some of the characters from the text. However, when attempting to comment in greater detail, such as in (19a, c), the learner could only report in the present tense, suggesting that she did not control the more specific content of the text to any great extent.

EPISTEMIC STANCE

Speakers express their attitudes regarding the truth value of their statements by the use of certain metacomments, modals and vague language (Frawley & Lantolf, 1985; DiCamilla & Lantolf, 1994). Use of these devices allows the speaker to distance herself from information she is not entirely sure of. In the case at hand, it is reasonable to assume that the language of the original text contributed heavily to the writers' uncertainty as to the meaning that they had constructed at the time of writing.

Metacomments

The excerpts in (20) and (21) illustrate the prototypical metacomment introduced by "I think" and provide evidence that the learners in these examples were working from the level of belief as opposed to absolute certainty (DiCamilla & Lantolf, 1994).

(20)   The bill concerned money for defense. <u>I think</u> that it had something to do with emposing [sic] some sort of trade restrictions on Cuba [...] [105A]
(21)   The act involves 247,000 millions of dollars and thirty countries. <u>I think</u> it forbids US subsidies to countries who support Fidel. [123A]

In the same way, the question mark in (22) expresses a degree of doubt on the part of the writer:

(22)   The article stated that the Bill ~~was an act of~~ acted to increase the strife of Cubans
       trying to apply for citizenship? [109 A]

This example is particularly interesting because it reveals a gradual, yet definitive, shift in the learner's orientation to the truth value of her writing. According to Givón's (1982) theory of propositions, the evidential "The article stated" indicates that this excerpt was initially presented with some measure of confidence on the part of the writer. However, the learner then struggled through the writing of the proposition, crossing out several words, until she ultimately was able to finish the sentence. These features clearly suggest that the learner was engaged in meaning-making, as opposed to merely meaning-relating. The question mark, however, indicates that the learner was not entirely convinced of the statement at which she had arrived. Thus, her assessment of its truth value went from confident to doubtful, as she was writing.

Epistemic Modality

The modals "will," "can," and, "would" were often used to express the learners' propositional attitudes. This can be clearly seen in the following excerpt (23a-e):

(23)   a.   The President of the United States, George Bush, enacted a law
       b.   which would set up an embargo against Castro's regime in Cuba.
       c.   This would be in protest to Castro's communist philosophy [....]
       d.   Bush hopes to set up a trade alliance with Canada, Mexico and, France.
       e.   The support of these countries would put more economic pressure on Castro.
            [114A]

The first proposition in the protocol (23a) was written in past tense, indicating that the learner was sure that a law had been enacted. However, in the following proposition (23b) the modal "would" is used. It is possible that the learner was expressing a degree of uncertainty as to the specifics of the bill. This hypothesis seems confirmed by the use of the same modal in the following line (23c), which attempts to explain the motivation behind (23a). The information in (23c) is not in the original text, and it must have come from the learner's own background knowledge which he used to justify what he understood of the text. The fact that the learner needed to justify the information contained in (23b) strongly suggests that he was not certain of it. Nor was he entirely sure of the verification (23c), as the modal indicates. This pattern repeats itself in the last lines of the recall (23d, e).

Vague Language

A further characteristic of the recall protocols for the Spanish newspaper text, related to the problem of truth value, is the use of vague language. Channell (1994) proposes that often times vague language is used when speakers lack specific information or are uncertain about what they are saying, and furthermore wish to distance themselves from what they are saying. Thus, like the use of modals and metacomments, vague language allows speakers to express information without committing themselves too strongly to its truth value.

In the recall protocols there are several sentential patterns involving vague or missing information. Declarative sentences can be thought to contain both a topic and a comment. In the recall protocols, it is frequently the case that one of these items is vague or lacking. At times, the learners appeared to possess topic information about which they could not comment, or could comment on only vaguely, while at others, the learners appear to have comment-like information about a topic for which they had no name. In these instances, vague language serves as a place holder, providing a structure or a scaffold through which the learners can construct the information they do have.

The learners employed a number of set phrases in order to introduce certain topics without having to elaborate on them. In (24a) we find a presentational sentence, containing the existential construction "there were," by which the writer was able to express the topic "petitions." However, the learner in (24) produced no true comment regarding this topic, and simply went on to present a second one, "Canada and France" by using the vague phrase "were involved" without further comment. Thus, the entire sentence given in (24a-b) is actually nothing more than a list of topics. In (25) and (26) we find examples of another phrase used by learners in order to present topics.

(24)   a.   There were petitions and
          b.   France and Canada were involved. [113A]
(25)   France and Mexico were also mentioned. [105A]
(26)   600 city dwellers were mentioned in this. [118A]

The presence of these presentational structures is important because it indicates that these learners were oriented to the task such that it implied producing writing complete sentences, in spite of the fact that these sentences contained little information.

Sometimes the learners commented on a topic, but only in a very general way (27):

(27)   George Bush [....] signed a law concerning Cuba. [...] The bill concerned money for defense. I think that it had something to do with emposing [sic] some sort of trade restrictions on Cuba. [105A]

Here, the underlined expressions introduce a comment that only vaguely modifies the topic. The lack of specificity in the comment suggests that the learner did not have a deep or detailed understanding of the information therein, nor its precise relationship to the topic.

Finally, phrases such as "some" and "something," as well as blank spaces, were used frequently in the protocols, apparently in order to compensate for missing or incomplete topic information. Used as placeholders, these devices allowed learners to express what information they had, and thus produce more or less complete sentences. This occurred frequently in the case of proper names. Examples (28-30) illustrate several ways in which vague language was used to compensate for the learners' not knowing the full names of the legislators mentioned in the article.

(28)   The man who drafted the law and another senator were not invited [...] [103A]
(29)   There were two senators who opposed this act, one from New Jersey and the other from Florida. [111A]
(30)   [...] democrat ~~Bob~~ Robert Torricelli (rep from   ) + Bob _____, senator from Florida. [204A]

In (28) and (29), the learners referred to the senators in question in an imprecise way, as indicated by the underlined phrases. However, the use of the determiner "the" in (28) implies that the learner treated the information "man" as given and specific. Thus, for the writer, the referent was not vague. In fact, although the learner was not able to provide the state nor the names of the senators, she was able to report that they were uninvited. With the use of "one" and "the other" in (29), again lacking the names of the legislators, the learner was able to provide information concerning where they were from, and their position regarding the new law. In (30), the writer clearly signaled that he lacked information, but, by leaving blank spaces, he was able to build a structure for what meaning he was able to construct.

Channell (1994) has found that speakers additionally use vague language in order to mark information, not as true or false, but as representative. Through the use of tags such as "or something like that" or "and stuff like that" speakers establish vague or general categories of which an item is a good example. Consider for instance, the request in (31):

(31)   Bring me a bagel or something.

In this case, the exemplar "bagel" has been followed by the tag "or something," thus forming what Channell (1994) refers to as a vague category identifier (p. 122). This should be understood as a clue for the listener to interpret the speaker as wanting, not necessarily a bagel per se, but something that belongs to the same general, but perhaps unnamed, category, which may, for example, include other items such as muffins or doughnuts.

Vague categories are often constructed for those categories which can be shown to exist but which lack a name, also known as "common categories" (Channell, 1994, p. 123). One example of a common category may be "the class of food items that you are likely to find at the student union coffee shop and that would be good for a quick lunch," as could be the case of (31). Vague categories may also represent "ad hoc categories," which do not enjoy the same cognitive status as common categories, and may only "come into existence for a person according to the demands of the moment" (Channell, 1984, p. 122-123).

What is of interest to the present discussion is what the construction of ad hoc categories can say about a speaker's epistemic stance regarding certain information. Consider the following examples (32-33):

(32)   [...] Bush signed the bill (law) called the Tocelli [sic] Law (or something like that) [205A]

(33)   George Bush wants to have a compact or something of that sort. [...] [125A]

In (32), the learner created a vague category by attaching the tag "or something like that" to the exemplar, "the bill (law) called the Tocelli law."[8] In (33), the learner did the same by attaching "or something of that sort" to the exemplar "compact." The evidence suggests that the learner portrayed in (32) was uncertain of the item he mentioned. For example, he hesitated between calling it a law or a bill, and apparently did not know the correct spelling. It seems reasonable to posit, then, that, in both (32) and (33), the on-line creation of an ad hoc category was meant to compensate for the writers' uncertainty about the items under discussion. In effect, then, the learner in (32) offered what she felt was a reasonable approximation to the name of the bill, but, importantly, she also marked it as only such. Thus, the tag functions almost as a disclaimer, allowing the learner to give information without committing to its truth value.

REFERENCE

Ambiguous pronominal reference, abbreviation, focus and externalization are features of the recall protocols that seem to relate to the same, larger issue, that is, how much information is made explicit by the writer and why? At times, the learners appear to construct too little information, so that for the reader, the discourse is ambiguous and confusing. At others, they retain and repeat lengthy forms which otherwise could have been abbreviated or even suppressed. Researchers working in Sociocultural Theory have shown that both phenomena (ambiguity or abbreviation and redundancy) are indicative of private writing and the cognitive needs of the writer to construct meaning.

Abbreviation and elaboration, in general, are characteristic of both social and private speech. However, the difference seems to lie in the criteria for expressing and suppressing information. Social speech is communicatively oriented and the emphasis is placed on being, for the listener's benefit, maximally informative (avoid ambiguity) and minimally redundant (be brief) (Grice, 1975). The communicative goals of socially oriented speech often requires that given and new information be marked differently and that topics be distinguished from one another. Thus, the perceived needs of the listener constitute the criteria for the amount of information externalized in social speech.

Private speech, on the other hand, is self-oriented and does not take the other entirely into consideration at the moment of producing discourse. Thus, the amount of information in private discourse is not determined by a communicative orientation. In private speech, then, topics do not always need to be distinguished from each other in the discourse, at least in theory, because the speaker ought always to know who or what she is talking about. Thus, the degree of overtness in private writing is determined by the writer's own need for distinction, and may appear to violate restrictions on ambiguity. The amount of information expressed or the way in which information is constructed, then, reflects the status of the item with respect to the writer's attention in the on-line process of meaning-making (Frawley, 1992). Unimportant or unfocused information is simply not expressed to the extent the language will allow, or is suppressed by using pronouns, vague language and other abbreviations. In contrast, important information, or information under construction, perhaps because of difficulty, will be made explicit, often repeatedly, in private speech. Thus, the need to externalize information ought to violate communicative requirements of being brief.

It is important to point out that both orientations, communicative and problem-solving, are essentially dialogic in nature. The fundamental difference is that social speech is directed at an "other" who, while not necessarily present, is someone other than the self. In private speech, on the other hand, the "other" is merely symbolic in that it is, in fact, the self. In large part, then, it is the identity of the other which determines the orientation and thus the linguistic properties of speech. Of course, the distinction between the self and the other, as the data from this study show, is not categorical, and speakers may be both self- and other-oriented at different points in the activity.

Unmarked Shifts in Reference

Frawley & Lantolf (1985) were the first to show that the way in which speakers use pronominal reference may be indicative of their cognitive state in the task and their level of control. Particularly, they have found that ambiguous reference suggests that the speaker is not entirely in control of her relating of the discourse.[9] As a result, the speaker (or in this case, the writer) produces discourse in an attempt to make the self the locus of control, and thus does not, or cannot, conform to the traditional communicative norms mentioned above. Unlike the private speech features discussed thus far, it is not clear that ambiguous reference has a specific strategic value. McCafferty (1994b) has argued that it is not obvious how being ambiguous can actually help one achieve control of the discourse (p. 425). However, because the production of ambiguous reference does seem to reflect the speaker's inner order, revealing a lack of control and an orientation toward creating meaning using discursive tools, it seems appropriate that it remain a category of private speech.

Pronominal reference can be ambiguous, for example, as a result of the continued pronominalization of thematic characters despite shifts in reference.[10] This phenomenon manifested itself robustly in the Spanish newspaper recall protocols and can be seen in examples (34-35):

(34)   George Bush [...] He worked towards helping convert countries (Cuba) towards democracy. By prohibiting subsidies amounting to hundreds of millions of dollars towards third world countries supporting Fidel Castro, he hoped to dissuade them from helping his regime. [121A]

(35)   It was dated October 28 . [127A]

In (34), the possessive pronoun "his" in "his regime" seems to refer to Castro in spite of the fact that the immediately preceding pronominal reference in the same sentence, "he," refers to George Bush. The sentence in (35) was the last sentence of the recall and apparently referred back to the article itself, which, although mentioned at the start of the recall, had not been mentioned since.

On one occasion, the learner modified a proposition, seemingly in order to avoid ambiguity (36).

(36)   Bush declares that he will not rest [...] Castro must fall. [...] ^A Representative from New Jersey and a senator were there, uninvited. He Bush is doing all he can to bring about the fall of Fidel Castro. [113A]

If left unchanged, the referent of the pronoun "he" would have been unclear, and perhaps could have been understood as referring to either of the two legislators mentioned, as well as to George Bush. However, this learner was sufficiently in control of the task at some point, that she was able to recognize and resolve the ambiguity.[11] The correction, then, reveals a shift from self-orientation to other-orientation.

Like personal pronouns, deictic pronouns were used in spite of little evidence in the recall with which an outsider could identify an antecedent. An example of this can be seen below where the antecedent of the underlined "this" (either the bill or the signing of the bill, presumably) is so distant that there are several, closer, potential antecedents (such as Torricelli's support of the bill, or the even amount of money was involved) (37):

(37)   Bush informed Miami of "Ley Torricelli" designed to "unite all of Cuba" into one free democracy.
       The act included $237,000 of military aid to support the overthrow of Castro. Torricelli is one of the act's prime supporters.
       There was much controversy over this, especially since it was before the elections and he wanted the Miamian cuban [sic] vote. [116A]

The above protocol contains an ambiguous personal pronoun as well. The pronoun "he" likely refers to President Bush, the first name listed. Yet, since the first mention of Bush, the names "Castro" and "Torricelli" have intervened and pragmatically, "Torricelli" is a possible antecedent for the pronoun. Such widespread ambiguity (for the reader) suggests that this particular learner was encountering considerable difficulty in constructing meaning and producing the recall.

Several protocols were further rendered confusing by the use of exophoric reference (38-39):

(38)   600 city dwellers were mentioned in this. [118 A]

(39)   Miami, Florida, US. October 28. President George Bush in the final days of his electoral campaign worked towards helping the people of Cuba heritage that lived there. [121A]

The pronoun "this" in (38) seems to refer to the original newspaper article itself, although it was never mentioned during the course of the recall. For the writer, however, the text was apparently present enough to be treated as given information, probably because it was the focus of much of her mental activity. In (39), the use of the "there" to refer to Miami, Florida would seem odd in a discourse with an entirely communicative purpose. The antecedent, although mentioned in the dateline, and certainly present in the mind of writer, is not mentioned in the recall text proper. Again, this odd pronominalization is evidence that the learner was not in sufficient control of the discourse to be able to present it in a communicative manner.

Focus and Externalization

Focus is a feature of private speech first discussed by Frawley (1992) in an L1 (cross linguistic) study of linguistic mediation that appears to complement the ambiguous and alternating use of reference described above. Frawley showed that, when faced with a cognitive problem, speakers continue referring to the same item without changing topic. As opposed to being ambiguous, then, the resulting discourse appears redundant. According to Frawley, this phenomenon occurs when, for whatever reason, the topic is the object of the speaker's ongoing mental activity. Focus can be realized through the repeated mention of a full noun phrase or pronoun without recourse to the strategies that the language permits in order to avoid redundancy (such as pronominalization, coordination and ellipsis), as can be seen in (40) below:

(40)   a.   The law called Rotticelli [sic] was recently passed
       b.   by Bush in October ^(**Friday 23**)
       c.   with the support of Robert Roticelli [sic] from New Jersey.
       d.   It is a very controversial law.

e. And some guy from Florida.
f. It will get rid of the trade embargo between Cuba and the United States.
g. It will get rid of the taxes also [....] [107A]

This example clearly shows that the writer had focused much of her attention on the law first mentioned in (41a). It seems reasonable to posit that this learner repeatedly directed her mental activity at a specific aspect of the text in an attempt to construct meaning. Repetition, then, is a semiotic device by which focus is maintained. Apparently this strategy was successful in this case, as the learner was able to generate more details about the nature of the item under focus. The resulting discourse does appear chaotic, if taken from a strictly communicative point of view. However, the language of this protocol is better understood as a working out in writing of a specific mental task, that is, as private writing.

The linguistic properties of the excerpt in (40) are consistent with what has been seen thus far, especially in the production of macrostructures, in which learners externalized information about the text in an attempt to know it, grasp it, think about it and analyze it. For Vygotsky, private speech represents the externalization of inner speech, of our consciousness: people externalize their linguistically mediated mental processes, in order to gain more control over them. Thus, we use external semiotic devices as kind of a scaffold to facilitate the recall or comprehension of additional information, in order to be able to carry out our meaning-making activity.

The protocols were rich in examples of externalization. There were several instances where externalization was a strategy for overcoming the language (Spanish) of the task, the most striking of which is presented in below (41):

(41) l
      m
      mier
      j
      viernes [109 A]

Writing in the margin of the recall text, this learner externalized a successful attempt to decipher the word *viernes*, "Friday" which appeared in the original text. Apparently, this learner knew that *viernes* was a day of the week, but was unsure as to which one. Thus, she executed a lexical search (in order to achieve a newly-formed subgoal) by writing down the days of the week one by one until arriving at *viernes*, the fifth day of the week: Friday.[12] This example is particularly illustrative of the strategic and cognitive value of external semiotic mediation.[13] It is also reminiscent of the common practice of language learners of copying down entire verbal paradigms in the corner of exam pages. This is usually information known to the students at a metalevel, but apparently only available for use if in an externalized, tangible form.

In the following example, seen earlier, the externalization of information in the macrostructure (the dateline) apparently allowed the learner to gain control over the language of the newspaper article and thus facilitated the construction of the subsequent proposition (42).

(42)   28 Octubre.
       On October 28, George Bush [....] [122A]

A further example of the value of externalization can be seen in those instances where learners produced propositions that show an increase in detail towards the end. That is, the learners started off with general information and perhaps due to the initial externalization of the topic were able to add more detail (43-44):

(43)   Bush signed a bill into law called the Torrecelli [sic] Law. [120 A]
(44)   A legislator from the state of Florida with the last name Graham. [118A]

Both (43) and (44) are alike in that the learner first mentioned a topic and then generated the proper name for each case. It is conceivable that if the learners had been conscious of the individual names at the time they began writing these lines, the sentences may have had a different form, such as the following (45-46):[14]

(45)   Bush signed the Torricelli bill into law.
(46)   Graham, a legislator from Florida [....]

ON-LINE EDITING

In the previous section it was shown that writing about the text, that is, constructing information about the text using external semiotic tools, led to comprehension on the part of the learners. While researchers often claim that written recall summaries are the reflection or externalization of what has been comprehended at the time of reading, the protocols here show that comprehension occurs during the recall task itself through the process of semiotic mediation.

The idea that writing facilitates both control of the task and comprehension of the text is further evident in those instances where learners realized "on-line editing" of the recall text. Learners often altered what they had previously written, going back and making changes, based, presumably on a new and perhaps contradictory interpretation of the text that emerged during the writing process. These changes are further evidence that comprehension of the original text can continue at the time of writing the recall protocol (Appel & Lantolf, 1994). Thus, writing a recall protocol involves the on-going creation and assignment of meaning, as was argued in Chapter 1.

In the following examples, the learners replaced certain propositions with others, apparently immediately after writing them, (47-48):

(47) On Friday October 23?Bush signed the Torricelli Act (now a law) banning all ~~third world countries~~ US Subsidiary companies housed in 3rd world countries from trading w/ Cuba. [101A]

(48) ~~law~~ act [116A]

Here the learners altered the text by crossing out and replacing a given proposition in order to reflect a new interpretation that arose presumably while, or after, the first interpretation was written. Furthermore, the writer in (47), while not scratching out her initial characterization of "Act," does add a clarification to what she had originally written ("now a law"). These examples are curious in that they reflect the confusion felt by many of the learners regarding the nature of the legislation involved. Specifically, they were unsure of how to refer to the Torricelli law, which they thought had originally been a bill or an act. In general, the learners seem to have shown a preference for using "bill" or "act" while referring to the actual signing, and "law" for talking about other aspects, such as its consequences. In the newspaper article itself, the legislation was only referred to as the Ley Torricelli "Torricelli Law." Apparently adding to the confusion was the presence of the word actos "acts" in the original text, although it referred to the actions of George Bush, and not NSspecifically to the law.

In other cases, the writing of the text seemed to indicate that the editing had taken place at some later time. That was true of those instances where the new information appeared in a different part of the recall text but was directed toward the replaced item by an arrow, or, as in (49-51), where the change appeared above the crossed out item:

(49) there are over 600,000 ~~Cubans~~ ^**Cuban Americans** living in Florida now. [117A]

(50) ~~law~~ ^**bill** [126A]

(51) [....Bush] ~~believes~~ ^**hopes** that someday all countries will be democratically run. [126 A]

Figure 3.1 shows various attempts at re-editing a single proposition.

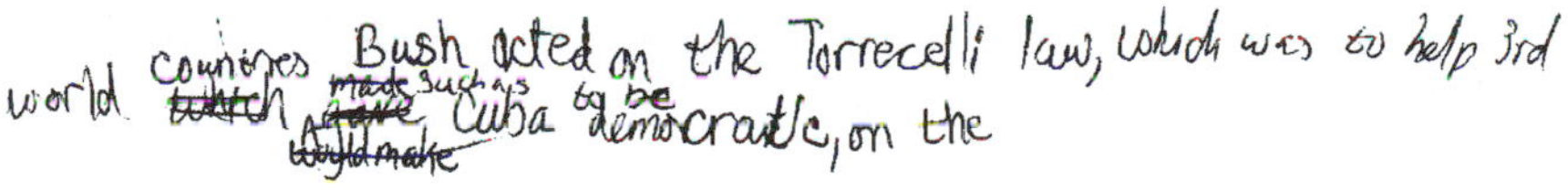

FIGURE 3.1

The writing in Figure 3.1 suggests the following derivation (52):

(52)   a.   Bush acted on the Torrecelli [sic] law, which gave Cuba democrac
       b.   Bush acted on the Torrecelli [sic] law, which ~~gave~~ ^**made** Cuba democractic
       c.   Bush acted on the Torrecelli [sic] law, which gave ^~~**made**~~ ^*would make* Cuba democraetic
       d.   Bush acted on the Torrecelli [sic] law ^*which was to help third world countries* ~~which gave would make~~ ^**such as** Cuba ^**to be** democraetic

To arrive at the proposition in (52d), the learner crossed out, replaced, modified and re-integrated several items that he had already written. It is clear that the learner did not modify a mere detail, as might be said of the editing in (47-51), but rather reworked and re-analyzed an entire proposition. It is curious that with all the complicated changes that this learner made, he did not simply scratch out the entire sentence and start anew. That he did not do so strongly suggests that the writing on the page was of real importance to him in the editing process. That is to say that this learner was actually working with the ideas as they were externalized and made tangible as words on paper, while he attempted to make sense out of the text. Vygotsky has said that writing is a "conversation with a white piece of paper" (John-Steiner, 1985b, p. 348). Figure 3.1 is such a conversation with the self.

Unlike Appel & Lantolf's (1994) findings, the "illusion of comprehension" was not a feature of the protocols of the Spanish newspaper text. Drawing on the work of Smirnov (1973), Appel & Lantolf discovered that readers often overestimate the extent to which they have understood a passage and are later confronted with this erroneous assessment at the time of recall. In the oral recall protocols of their study this confrontation was often, but not always, signaled by metacomments such as "I forgot" and a clear shift in orientation. There were no such instances in the written Spanish recall protocols. One possibility is that the written nature of this particular task was sufficient to inhibit the learners' metacomments. However, we might expect the illusion of comprehension to show up in other ways as well, such as in the language of the text or in instances of on-line editing.[15] Thus, a better explanation for the absence of this feature might lie in the fact that the illusion of comprehension depends on the learners' having initially deceived themselves as to how much they understood of the text. It is very likely that these learners were fairly aware of the difficulties that this particular text posed to them and, accordingly, did not harbor any illusions as to how well they had comprehended it.

SUMMARY

The analysis of the linguistic and discursive features of the recall protocols of the L2 newspaper text revealed abundant examples of private writing. The learners, faced with the difficult task of producing a recall protocol, were obliged to realize their meaning-constructing activity externally, even as they wrote a recall with a supposed communicative purpose, namely that of demonstrating how much of the text they had understood.

The presence of private writing was revealing of the difficulty that many learners encountered with the target text. Indeed on many occasions it was evident, through the language of the protocols, that the learners were simply overwhelmed by the task and the information in the text. Not surprisingly, the language of the task seemed to be the most towering problem facing the learners. The content of the protocols suggests that decoding the Spanish was indeed a real and sometimes insurmountable problem. In some cases, it was possible to see where writers were able to use private speech strategically, in order to get a grip on the task, construct meaning from what they had read, and, in general, complete the task.

Importantly, this analysis has begun to suggest ways in which private writing features can reveal information about the learner's orientation to and control of the task. The activity of producing a recall protocol is a complex one. It can involve not only the (re)creating of a substantial amount of information, but also getting started in the task, finding the right lexicon, and tying ideas together. For that reason, orientation—the way in which people view and plan to carry out a task—is an equally complex feature of this activity. Adding to that, as has been amply illustrated by the data, is the fact that orientation fluctuates as the task progresses. Thus, the task, as conceived of and carried out by individual learners, yields in each case a different activity. In Chapter 5, the concepts of orientation, task and activity will be discussed more fully, taking into account the data presented in the present chapter, as well as the data from the L1 recall protocols offered in the following chapter.

NOTES

[1]   L2 refers to the language of the experimental text, Spanish; the protocols were written in the learners' native language, English.

[2]   The learner's number is given in brackets: learners [101-127] are third semester, elementary students, learners [201- 205] are fifth semester, intermediate students. The letter following the learner number refers to the text: A = the Spanish newspaper text, B = the English newspaper text, C = the English Expository text.

[3]   The experiment was administered in early December, thus it is not likely that the writer could assume that the reader would understand the 28th to refer to the then current month.

⁴ That is, this learner is writing for himself and does not externalize information which is obvious and insignificant to him. This, then, is a potential problem for the assumption made by those who perform quantitative analysis of recall protocols that what is written was understood while what is missing was not.

⁵ The content of the recall, however, reveals that the writer, although in control of the information in the recall, was incorrect in his interpretation.

⁶ The present progressive is typically used in narratives to describe background information (i.e. with stative verbs) and actions that are about to be interrupted by the main action of the event. Interestingly, the present progressive is seemingly used to forward action only when what happens next is as yet unknown. Such is the case of sports reporting, for example, which is often no more than a sequence of chronologically ordered descriptions (i.e. He's wheeling back, he's looking for a receiver, he's throwing, etc.) (L. Waugh, private communication). The sports reporter is, of course, limited by her knowledge of the facts because they have not yet occurred. The learners in this study are limited because they have not understood what was reported to have occurred.

⁷ The instance of the present progressive in this excerpt (19 j) "They are going to block off trade" appears to be example of the periphrastic future.

⁸ It is possible of course that the exemplar is the whole sentence "Bush signed the bill" whereby the learner is unsure of Bush's actions. However, the confusion between "bill" and "law," and the misspelling of "Torricelli" suggest that the learner's difficulty lay with understanding precisely what it was that Bush signed.

⁹ The relative absence of control in the relating may be the result of a language problem, as was the case of Frawley and Lantolf's (1985) non-native subjects in the picture narration task; of the difficulty in constructing cohesive texts, such as Frawley and Lantolf's child L1 speakers in the same task; or it may be an information problem, in that the speaker or writer does not control the facts of the text, because they are being created in the act of speaking or writing, as in the case of the novice L1 writers in DiCamilla and Lantolf (1994).

¹⁰ Again, it is important to keep in mind that such language is ambiguous for the reader, but not for the writer at the time of writing. One possibility, not explored in this study, however, is that the language might be ambiguous for the writer-turned-reader at a later date.

¹¹ Since the writing of the protocols was not videotaped, it is impossible to know for sure when the learner made this adjustment, which may have occurred "on-line" or during a later editing phase. However, by looking at the protocol, we find that "Bush" was not squeezed in or written above "He," indicating that the change was made while there was still room in the writing to fit "Bush" in, that is, on-line.

¹² In the Spanish speaking world *lunes* "Monday" is considered the first day of the week, and it is in that order that most students of Spanish are taught the days of the week.

¹³ It is also a good example of the abbreviated nature of private speech. There is nothing redundant in this list—the learner externalized only what was absolutely necessary for her distinguish among the days of the week.

¹⁴ It is also possible that the frequent confusion between "bill" and "law" was responsible for some of the awkwardness in (43). By writing "signed," the learner was forced into following up with "bill." However, the "Torricelli bill" was never mentioned in the original

text, and thus it may very well have been "law" which prompted the use of the full title "Torricelli law."

[15]   As will be shown in the following chapter to be the case of recall protocols of the English language texts.

4

The L1 Protocols

This chapter examines the linguistic features of the recall protocols of the L1 texts, a newspaper article and an expository text in English. As with the recalls of the Spanish newspaper text in the previous chapter, the discussion will focus on the private speech features evident in the protocols—including macrostructure, tense and aspect, modality, reference, focus and externalization, as well as evidence of on-line editing—in the hope of discovering properties of the learners' activity and orientation as they proceeded through the task of reading and reconstructing two native language texts.

Unlike the Spanish newspaper article, it was assumed that the language of the two texts in English would not pose a problem for the learners because it was their native language. However, in both cases, the recall was expected to be a least somewhat difficult, given the relatively short time period that the learners were given to produce the written protocols. In the case of the expository text, the content, a discussion of physics, was expected to cause further difficulties for the learners.

MACROSTRUCTURE

The English Newspaper Text

Macrostructure has been defined as the writer's externalization of some information about the task or the text, whether it be through a label or a statement summarizing the gist of the text. Like the newspaper article in Spanish, the English newspaper article was headed by a title, a dateline and a summarizing lead sentence. Given these clues, it is not surprising that the learners produced one or more of these features at the beginning of the recall protocol. Some learners, for example, reproduced the dateline (1-2):[1]

(1)   Peru Nov 22 [103B]
(2)   Lima Peru Nov 22 [106B]

In addition to a dateline, many learners produced a title as part of their recall. Again, this orientation is suggested by the original text. Interestingly, the recall protocols of the English newspaper text exhibited more titles than the Spanish recall protocols. Moreover, these titles tended to be more elaborated and more closely resembled the title in the original text (3-5):

(3)   Fujimori seems to win in Peru [110B]
(4)   Fujimori seems to win in Peru, a voter survey says. [119B]
(5)   Fujimori wins over the ^support with the Peruvians. [124B]

Labeling the text with titles, such as those in (3-5), or a dateline (1-2) may not be an indication of difficulty but may represent an orientation to producing a recall which looked like the original text—a newspaper article. However, it is possible that the production of a macrostructure did allow the writers to gain a degree of control at the beginning of task.

Several learners produced labels that, unlike the examples (1-5) were not directly suggested by the text. Some labels seemed to indicate a lack of control at the outset of writing the protocol. An example is given in (6):

(6)   Takes place in Lima, Peru [118B]

The label in (6), was the first line written and apparently refers to the events reported on in the original text. For communicative purposes, this is an odd way of beginning a recall protocol, in that the label does not refer the reader specifically to the text being recalled. This is evidence that the learner was in engaged in primarily self-directed problem-solving activity.

Newspaper articles almost always begin with an abstract or summary component and, not surprisingly, several learners began the recall of the English newspaper text by first providing the gist of the article (7-10):

(7)   Strong support is shown for Alberto K. Fujimori. [110B]
(8)   Voter surveys showed Peruvians supported Pres. Fujimori's candidates for Congress [...] [103B]
(9)   There was a huge turnout and general support for Alberto Fujimori's candidates [...] [115B]

(11)   If the now President Fujimori wins the elections, he believes that it will show
        approval for his actions on April 5 when he seized power. [121B]

Most often, these abstracts appeared with a dateline and a title, and thus seemed to
reflect an orientation toward the faithful reproduction of the original text, including its physical properties. To some extent, the complexity of the summary statements allows us to distinguish between each recall. Compare, for example, the
lead in (7) with those in (8-10). The brevity of the lead in (7) is reminiscent of a
title. In contrast, the opening lines in (8-10) are complex and rich in detail, suggesting a greater degree of control on the part of the writer at the beginning of the
recall.
    One abstract in particular seemed to reveal the on-going cognitive process of
understanding the text (11):

(11)   Nov 22 Lima, Peru. Fujimoro [sic]—voter poll; in which it was found that the
        majority of Peruvians supported dictator Fujimoro's [sic] regime. [108B]

Like the examples in (7-10), the statement in (11) contains the main point of the
article, as constructed by the reader. However, this particular macrostructure is
highly abbreviated. There are no complete sentences, rather a collection of brief
but increasingly more detailed propositions. In fact, the whole series of information looks more like class notes, instead of a formalized macrostructure. Perhaps
more so than the others, this macrostructure was oriented at the writer instead of
the reader. The global meaning assigned by the reader to the experimental text was
externalized not to tell the reader what the text was about, but so the writer could
know what it was about.
    The following excerpts constitute a representative sample of the summary
macrostructures that were found in the recall protocols of English newspaper text
(12-14):

(12)   The newsarticle [sic] entitled about the quasi-dictator Fujimori in Peru reported
        that results of a poll taken of voters leaving voting places pointed towards his vict
        drafting a new constitution by 80 members of parliament. [109B]
(13)   This writing discussed how the present Peruvian president, Fujimore [sic],
        seemed to receive ^the majority support ^from his the people in his country in
        a voting on Nov. 22. [127B]
(14)   This is an article about the election in Peru on Nov. 22. [205B]

It is interesting to note that there were about the same number of summary macrostructures for the Spanish newspaper text as for the English newspaper text. This
suggests that the use of such a macrostructure in the recall of the newspaper texts
in this study does not necessarily indicate difficulty. The way in which the macrostructures were realized, however, is very revealing. For example, the macrostructures in (12-13) are rather elaborated, much more so than the summary

macrostructures found in the recalls of the Spanish newspaper text. This is not particularly surprising, and is presumably the result of the learners having understood more of the English newspaper text.

Finally, one learner began the recall as a narrative by employing a story-like opening (15):

(15)   It is Nov. 22 in Lima, Peru. [111B]

At this point, it is interesting to note that the learner began his recall of the Spanish newspaper article in a similar way. Further comment on this particular example will be saved for a later discussion, concurrent with the analysis of the tense/aspect features of the protocol.

The English Expository Text

The L1 expository text was, of course, very different from either of the newspaper texts, both in content as well as structure and style. The newspaper articles dealt with U.S. and Latin American political events and presented the same format, which included the presence of a title and dateline and an inverted structure in which a summary of the article was presented first, followed by background information and secondary details. In contrast, the expository text dealt with the problem of balance as it relates to the possibility of designing a machine to imitate walking. This text begins with a short title and a few introductory paragraphs, which, unlike the newspaper articles, do not summarize the main ideas of the text. The text then goes on at greater length to compare and contrast two different forms of balance. The structural differences between the two types of texts are reflected in the macrostructures produced for the expository texts.

As with the newspaper texts, titles headed several of the recalls of the expository text, although, as ought to be expected, there were no datelines. Examples of titles are given below (16-17):

(16)   Machines that Walk [121C]
(17)   Can ^we make machines that walk? [110C]

The title in (16) is brief, but is identical to the title of the original text. The title in (17) is interesting because, in addition to showing an on-line revision, it reveals that the learner had appropriated a question from within the body of the original text in constructing a title for the recall protocol. It suggests that her attention was focused specifically on the problem presented in the text, and that she had assigned the text that global meaning.

Two other learners began their recall protocols by making use of this question, not as a title, however, but in beginning the protocols (18-19):

(18)   Can humans use math & computer models to help build machines that walk or
       run? Airplanes show it is possible to make ones that fly. [116C]

(19)   Many machines imitate nature The airplane imitates the soaring bird could machines ever learn to walk as humans.
Research has shown that a horse does have all four off its legs of the ground [...]
[106C]

The question in (18) sums up the problem presented initially in the expository text. In contrast, the presence of a question in the second example (19) seems to indicate an orientation toward memorizing the original text, rather than to serve as a rhetorical device.[2] For example, it is not followed by an interrogative mark, and is only identifiable as a question because of the subject-verb inversion. The question is also neither answered nor made to fit cohesively into the surrounding discourse. Therefore, it appears that the writer was oriented toward copying the original text verbatim, focusing not on the meaning but on the words of the text. It is also likely that the learner did not even view the sentence as a question, but was instead oriented to appropriating entire phrases from the text. However, this orientation has left him ill-prepared to produce a cohesive recall text.

The expository text does not begin with a summarizing paragraph or sentence, but rather with an introductory comment that discusses the relationship of machines to animals, and the failure thus far to produce a machine capable of imitating walking. The second part of the text addresses what might be called the main topic of the text: the differences between two types of balance. The recall protocols for this text show two distinct trends in the organization of information in the recall protocols. Some learners began their recalls by discussing the introductory comment (20), while others went to the heart of the matter and began discussing balance (21):

(20)   Many machines imitate nature. [101C]
(21)   One big problem in designing machines that walk is in establishing dynamic balance whereby motion is computed with velocity taken into consideration. [122C]

Excerpt (20) matches exactly the opening line of the experimental text and perhaps reflects an orientation to reproduce. It is also possible that the brevity of the sentence somehow made it more salient for the learner and thus easier to remember. Again, it is not possible to determine why a learner would adopt one or the other orientation, yet one can comment on the relative degree of difficulty experienced by the learners by looking at the ways in which these two orientations were realized. Compare, for example the opening lines in (22-25):

(22)   Machines imitate. [125C]
(23)   Machines have often reflected nature in many ways. [102C]
(24)   Man has been able to build machines that imitate the locomotion patterns of animals. [105C]

(25)   There are many ways in which machines imitate animals and the other way around. [113C]

Again, the amount of detail and complexity allows us to distinguish between opening lines, with greater detail and complexity suggesting greater control. Length alone, however, does not necessarily indicate control, as the example in (25) seems to suggest.

One learner began her recall of the expository text in the same way in which she did the English newspaper text, that is with an abbreviated macrostructure which might better be thought of as notetaking (26):

(26)   Dynamics of walking so complex that not even computers can recreate the action through biofeedback. [108C]

Again, this writer assigns a global meaning to (i.e. labels) the text she has just read with a brief comment regarding its content. A similar private macrostructure was produced by another learner (27):

(27)   Motion is discussed as being xxxx able to be copied mechanically and then different types of locomotion—walking, opposed to running. [205C]

The macrostructure in (27) is initially somewhat more explicit and more complete than the one in (26). It begins as a complete sentence, which, while not mentioning the text directly, does allude to it through the phrase "is discussed." Ultimately, the macrostructure turns into an abbreviated list, suggesting an on-line change in orientation, in which cohesion is no longer a goal (or sub-goal) of the activity.

The recall protocols also contain a number of complete summary macrostructures, which like the opening lines, showed two distinct patterns—those referring to the initial comment (28-31) and those referring to the problem of balance (32-34).[3]

(28)   This article concerns the nature of walking and its relationship to machines. [107C]
(29)   The piece entitled "Machines that Walk" adressed [sic] the problem of trying to find create machines with the ability to walk [...] [109C]
(30)   The authors of this article wonder if modern technology can create machines to imitate walking motions. [114C]
(31)   According to the previous page, engineering efforts to mimic walking and in mechanical "robots" has been difficult at best. [124C]
(32)   Machines that walk deals with the two major differences between static and dynamic machines. [118C]
(33)   This writing, entitled "Machines That Walk" described different levels of stability that occur and need to occur [...] [127C]
(34)   This article, with all its sentences jumbled around dealt with balance and motion and animals. [203C]

An interesting feature of these macrostructures is that they all, with the exception of (34), incline toward one of the two topics touched upon in the text—the anecdote-like discussion of the relationship between machines and animal mobility, or the discussion of balance. The choice of topic is an interesting one and reveals something about the learner's reading of the text. Namely, it possibly indicates what the writers considered to be the most important, or perhaps, most salient part of the text. Ostensibly, it was a choice between what was mentioned first, and what was discussed at greater length, a decision very likely affected by how much the learners understood of each discussion. The macrostructure in (34) is perhaps the vaguest and most general of those given above, suggesting that the writer did not understand enough of either topic to expand on them.

Finally, while both sets of recall protocols exhibited summary macrostructures, there were more summary macrostructures present in the recall protocols of the expository text than those of the English newspaper article. Moreover, the recall protocols of the expository text showed greater variation in the form of the macrostructures. For example, as can be seen in (28-34), there are references to "the article," the "piece," the "authors," and even to "Machines that walk." One plausible explanation for the proliferation of summary macrostructures in the expository recalls might be that, on the whole, university students are much more likely to be asked to write about expository texts than newspaper articles. Furthermore, they are more likely to summarize such texts, as opposed to simply replicate them. Thus, the learners would already have a model or blueprint for summarizing the expository text on which they could base their activity.[4]

TENSE AND ASPECT

The English Newspaper Text

It is only appropriate to discuss the tenses of the recall protocols of the English experimental texts by first examining the pattern of tense and aspect in the original texts themselves. In general, the English newspaper article displays a more complicated pattern of tenses than either the Spanish newspaper text or the English expository text. Unlike the Spanish newspaper article which reported on a completed event—President Bush's visit to Miami—the English newspaper reports on an event which was not completed at the time of writing—congressional elections in Peru. This event and related circumstances (i.e. opposition to the elections) are accordingly reported on in the present tense. The potential consequences of the event (i.e. perceived legitimacy in the eyes of foreign governments) are presented via the future tense. Additionally, the English article goes on to provide background information about events which predate the elections (i.e. Fujimori's takeover of the government earlier in the year). These events, then, are reported on in the past tense. Thus, the English newspaper article shows a rather wide range of tense and aspect which needs to be taken into consideration when examining the recall protocols.

Two general trends can be found in the recall protocols of the English newspaper text. The first consisted of the predominant use of past tense, in which learners referred to the elections as already having taken place. For some reason, perhaps because of the date of the article (about 2 weeks prior to the time of the experiment), the learners treated the main events of the article as having been completed at the time of writing the protocols. This trend is seen in the following examples (35-36):

(35)   On November 22 in Lima Perú, there <u>were</u> national elections for a set of Congress people wanted by President Alberto K. Fujimori to write the Peruvian constitution. [102B]

(36)   Elections <u>were</u> held in Lima Peru for Alberto K. Fujimori's new congress. Although the elections <u>were</u> disputed, they will give the government a ~~stroger~~ stronger sense of legitimacy. [202B]

The use of the past tense in these examples shows that the writers were oriented toward treating these events as distant, and importantly, as having been completed, regardless of the manner in which they were described in the original text.

The second trend was the predominant use of the present tense, through which the learners referred to the elections as still taking place, as they had been at the time of the writing of the original newspaper text (37-38):

(37)   Nov. 22
President Fujimori of Peru <u>is</u> expected to win the elections today, ^**7 months** after he seized power by disbanding congress and the rest of the government [...] [122B]

(38)   Peru Nov. 22
Voter surveys showed Peruvians supported Pres. Fujimori's candidates for Congress, although it was still unclear whether Fujimori had won a Parliamentary Majority.
The election, 5 months after Fuj. [sic] seized dictatorial control and disbanded congress, <u>consolidates</u> his control of the government. The president sees victory as an endorsement of his measures since April [...] [103B]

The present tense, underlined in the above examples, suggests that the learners were oriented toward expressing the immediacy and the incomplete nature of the elections. Given the likelihood that that most learners understood that these events were in fact complete at the time of their reading the newspaper article, it remains to be explained why the learners might have adopted such an orientation.

In the case of the Spanish newspaper article, it was suggested that the use of the present tense in the protocols was evidence of difficulty and a lack of control. Thus, one possible explanation for this tense in the recalls of the English texts is that the learners were overwhelmed and trapped by the immediacy of the information in the English newspaper text, and thus presented the information in the present. However, because this text was in the learners' native language it seems unlikely that it would present them with a comparable amount of difficulty. A more likely explanation, which takes into account the present tense used in the original English newspaper text itself, is that the learners who used the present tense were oriented to reproducing the newspaper article as it appeared, thus using the semiotic devices given in the text, as opposed to reporting on the information in the text. This explanation seems confirmed by the apparent relationship between the use of the present tense and the presence of titles and datelines at the beginning of the protocol. By and large, the learners who produced datelines, or other features of the newspaper text, also referred to the elections as still taking place, as they had been described in the original text. Thus, these learners were more strongly oriented toward replicating the discursive structure of the original text, as opposed to reporting on the information contained within the text. An example of this orientation can be seen in the following excerpt (39):

(39)   Fujimori seems to win in Peru
        Lima, Peru, Nov. 22. Strong support is shown for Alberto K. Fujimori [...]But it
        is unclear whether he has the parliamentary support he sought [...] [110B]

In contrast, the learners who reported on the text in the past tense did not tend to produce datelines and the like and were those more likely to use summary macrostructures or to refer to the article (40):

(40)   This writing discussed how the present Peruvian president, Fujimore [sic],
        seemed to receive ^the majority support ^from the people in his country in a
        voting on Nov. 22 [...] [127B]

Additionally, several learners who were apparently oriented toward reporting on the events of the text, as opposed to replicating it, presented the information in the news article in chronological order instead of the order in which it appeared in the original text (41):

(41)   President Fugimori [sic] seized power ^of Peru April 5th and disbanded congress and the court, making giving him near dictatorial powers.
        Nov 22 was the election for the new 80-member congress. Several major parties
        refused to participate in the "illegal" election [...]
        Fugimori [sic] said that if the people he recommended for the posts congress won
        a majority, he'd take it as an indorsement [sic] of his April Activities [...] [123B]

It has already been pointed out that one of the major differences between personal narratives and news stories is that the latter always have an abstract component, while the former often do not. One of the consequences of having an abstract component, however, is that by presenting a summary of the main action before a description of background events and states, the events are not related in chronological order. However, if the abstract component is not realized, the resulting text, becomes chronological in its ordering, and more closely resembles a personal narrative. Thus, it is reasonable to argue that the writer, perhaps due to difficulty in producing a cohesive text, was not only not oriented toward reproducing the news article, but was more than likely oriented toward relating a story, in the familiar sense of the word.

The two predominant trends that have been presented here—reporting on and reproducing the original text—are important because they illustrate two very different, although arguably appropriate, orientations toward the task of recalling the newspaper article. Furthermore, the two distinct trends reveal how the same orientation may be manifested consistently throughout the protocols. In some cases, a given orientation was reflected in several features of the protocol, such as the tense and aspect, as well as the macrostructure.

In spite of this consistency there is some evidence in the data that at times the orientation adopted at the outset was not sustained throughout the protocol. For example, one learner who was apparently oriented toward reporting on the completed and thus distant events of the article, nonetheless allowed a present tense description of the events to slip into her recall, suggesting that she found her initial orientation too difficult to maintain (42):

(42)   In Lima, Peru on Nov. 22, there was an election for a congress that would rewrite
       the Peruvian constitution. This came about because [...] Fujimori disbanded the
       congress & the courts & destroyed the Constitution [...] Even though some large
       parties aren't participating in this 'illegitimate' election [...] [101B]

Interestingly, there were no examples of learners who exhibited the reproduction orientation employing the past tense inappropriately.[5] The evidence, while not overwhelming, suggests that this orientation was, at least for this task, the easier of the two, since it involved the reproduction of the information in the text as it appeared. On the other hand, the orientation toward reporting on the text involved the additional activity of temporally distancing oneself from the events in the original article, in the face of the force of the present in which they were related.

In spite of the fact that the text was in the learners' native language, there were several cases in which it was clear from the tenses that learners experienced difficulty. In one case, the present progressive indicated the struggle for control. While it is true that the events reported on in the article can be and have been described in the protocols as incomplete, the present progressive (as opposed to the present) is not an appropriate tense for expressing this incompleteness. The present progressive, as was argued in the preceding chapter, is often used in the description of unrelated information, but not in the relating of connected events. Consider, for example, the following excerpt (43):

(43)   Takes place in Lima Peru
Alberto Fujimori seize the government of Peru in April. Now in November elections <u>are being held</u> to elect an 80 person congress. Fujimori <u>is trying</u> to rewrite the peruvian [sic] constitution. If Fujimori receive a mayority [sic] of the vote, he feels that will be a sign that he did the right thing [...] Also he <u>is hoping</u> that other countries will recognize him as the ruler if his people support him. Guerrillas threatened to disrupt the election [...] [118B]

Here, the use of the present progressive, the list-like nature of the recall, and the label-like macrostructure "takes place" all suggest that the learner was for the most part oriented toward describing a static situation and not toward the retelling of related events. Therefore, it seems plausible to argue that the learner adopted this orientation due to difficulties with the task. The difficulty apparently did not lie in understanding the individual propositions of the text, as this protocol contains much information. Rather, it appears to have lain in integrating the information into a cohesive and coherent narrative. The present progressive indicates that the writer was constructing meaning on-line, never quite sure of what would follow. Thus, integration was impossible.

Finally, as was remarked in the preceding section, one learner apparently treated the newspaper text as a story (44):

(44)   It is Nov. 22 in Lima, Peru. Alberto K. Fujimori has decided to have the Peruvian constitution rewritten. However, he wasn't too sure of the congress' position on his plan, therefore he decided to hold elections to decide the outcome of the new constitution. This happen [sic] 7 months after Fujimori seized power in an almost dictatorial manner.
If this referendum were to be passed it would add legitimacy to his ~~his~~ presidency and prove that the people backed his initial seizing of power. [111B]

It is interesting to note that the learner began his recall of the Spanish newspaper article in the same way, suggesting that this individual preferred this particular strategy. This story-like introduction does not seem appropriate for the task at hand and probably indicates a control problem. Nonetheless, it is significant that in both cases the learner was able to continue the recall at some point in a more appropriate manner. In fact, the English newspaper recall, like the Spanish recall, shows a great deal of detail, as well as a suitable use of tense and aspect further in the recall. This suggests that the learner's difficulty might have been located in simply beginning the recall, as opposed to actually recalling the text. Thus, the strategy of producing a story-like opening may reflect an orientation toward gaining control at the outset of the task, by borrowing a more familiar discursive opening. In the case of this learner, it was apparently successful.

The English Expository Text

The use of tense and aspect in an expository text is a different than what is found in narrative texts. The expository text from this study represents a straightforward description and discussion of the problem of balance, and for the most part is realized with the present tense. There is but one reference to an event, which is related in the past, but this is only a minor departure from the central ideas of the text, which cannot be interpreted as a narrative. The recall protocols reflected this straightforwardness, and most were written primarily in the present tense (45-46)

(45) Machines often <u>imitate</u> nature, as airplanes imitate birds. Walking, however, <u>hasn't</u> been imitated by machine, but computer models <u>are</u> now <u>trying</u> to determine if this can be done.
       Studies done a century ago <u>show</u> that horse and humans as well as other animals completely <u>leave</u> the ground during running. The body <u>is</u> able to keep itself balanced using ballistic movements. [...]...[103C]
(46) One big problem in designing machines that walk <u>is</u> in establishing dynamic balance, whereby motion <u>is computed</u> with velocity taken into consideration [...] [122C]

The use of the present tense in these protocols suggests an orientation toward reproducing the information as it appeared in the original text. However, some recalls made reference to the authors and the text using the present tense. This suggests that for descriptive, scientific discourse, such as this expository text, an orientation toward reporting on the text does not require the same back shift in tense that was observed in the reporting orientation of the English newspaper protocols (47-48):

(47) This article <u>concerns</u> the nature of walking... it mainly <u>discusses</u> [107C]
(48) The authors of this article <u>wonder</u> if modern technology can create machines to imitate walking motions.
       One of their concerns <u>is</u> balance [...] [114C]

However, a back shift can not be said to be precluded either, as there were several instances of this, although they were restricted to references to the text or author, as the following examples show (49-51):

(49) This writing, entitled "Machines that walk," <u>described</u> different levels of stability [...] [127C]
(50) The piece [...] <u>addressed</u> [...] [109C]
(51) ~~Since m~~Man has built machines that imitate ^**almost all** the actions of animals such as an airplane that flys [sic] like ^**a** bird, except walking and running. The author ~~xxxx~~ <u>tried</u> to find if this were possible through the use of computers. He also <u>used</u> the fact that while running humans and other animals leave the ground... [104C]

The examples of past tense in the summary macrostructures in (49-50) as well as those in (51) which describe the author's actions, show that the learners treated the text as an event, instead of an entity.

EPISTEMIC STANCE

As they did with the Spanish text, learners writing about the two English experimental texts used metacomments, modals, and vague language to express their uncertainty about what they had read or what they were writing. Examples of each will be presented here. It is important to note that, overall, there were markedly fewer examples of epistemic modality at the sentence level (as opposed to the word level) in the recall protocols of the English texts than in the Spanish recall. This suggests that at the macrolevel, there was arguably less uncertainty about what they had read in the native language (English) texts.

Metacomments

There was a single example of a metacomment, which is given below (52):

(52)   This congress, which would have 80 members, would be established anyway I think because the article says the vote was only to prove to opposing forces that the country supports the new regime [...] [203B]

In this excerpt the learner expresses a degree of doubt via the evidential "I think." It is interesting to note that, in the only example of a metacomment from the L1 protocols, the learner cast doubt on an inference made based on the information in the text but not explicitly stated.

The interrogative sign in the recalls also reveals doubt on the part of the writer (53-55):

(53)   Eadward [sic] Baybridge? [125C]
(54)   Eadweard Mayberry [sic] in the late 19th (?) century [109C]
(55)   Statistical (?) stability is [...] [127 C]

It is interesting to observe that in these instances, the question marks fall not at the end of a sentence, but rather after certain words. This would seem to indicate that the uncertainty expressed referred, not to the entire sentence, but to the word or words immediately preceding the question mark.[6]

Quotation marks were frequently found in the recalls of both English texts, although more so for the expository text than the newspaper article. This seems to have been another way in which writers encoded uncertainty with regard to specific words or phrases, as opposed to entire sentences (56-61):

(56)   A "Fair voting agency" [108B]
(57)   a "still" camera [104C]
(58)   At some point [...] the organism is "tipping" [105C]
(59)   This also deals with the 'tipping' idea. [125C]
(60)   [...] as the vehicle is 'crawling' along. [118C]
(61)   For a car to remain balanced during stability it must be "on a tripod". [119C]

There were more question and quotation marks in the two English recalls than in the recall protocols of the Spanish text. However, it would be erroneous to jump to the conclusion that reading the English texts posed more difficulty than reading the text in Spanish. As was said in the previous chapter, it was apparent from the propositional content of the Spanish recall protocols that many learners had only little access to the content of the text. Most were not able to understand it at a sentence level, but rather were forced to create meaning based on the scattered words that they did understand (or believed they understood).

On the other hand, learners reading the English texts were likely to understand not only the majority of the words, but also the sentences, at least at a syntactic level. Apparently, some words did cause some difficulty (i.e. "Muybridge") or at the least the usage of some of them seemed surprising (i.e. "tipping," "statistical"). However, because of what learners did understand, we can assume that these words were not always critical to the construction of larger units of meaning. In fact, it might have been precisely the ability to form larger units easily that allowed the learners the luxury of wondering and commenting about the words that seemed odd to them.

Epistemic Modality

The modal "would" and the verb "seem" were used, this time only on occasion, to express doubt and uncertainty about the truth value of statements in the recall protocols. However, it is important to bear in mind that in the English newspaper text itself, there was some uncertainty expressed regarding the results of the then ongoing elections. In fact, the title states that "Fujimori seems to win in Peru." Thus, it is not surprising to find some doubt expressed in the recall protocols, as it is below through the use of the verb "seem" (62):

(62)   President Alberto K. Fujimori seems to have won the elections [...] [204B]

However, much of the information presented in the English newspaper text was given as certain, and thus, any doubt in the recall concerning that information must have come from the learner's own propositional attitude toward what she read. Consider then the use of "seem" in the following excerpt (63):

(63)   According to a recent survey, many Peruvians seem to support Mr. Fujimori as a candidate [...] 7 months ago in April, Fujimori seemed to gain dictatorial control [...] He believed that his action seemed to instigated support [...] [107B]

The first use of "seem" in (63) is justified, because it refers to information presented as uncertain or yet-to-be-known in the original text. However, the second and third uses are odd, in that they refer to past events presented as certain. Thus, "seem" likely reflects doubt, not in the text, but in the mind of the learner regarding what she had read. Consider also, then, the following examples (64-65):

(64)   Many people who were willing to comment showed support of Fujimori [120B].
(65)   Those who responded [...] seemed to support Fujimari [sic]. [117B]

Again, while the results of the elections were not yet known, the results of the polls were certain, as stated in (64). Thus, the hesitation in (65), expressed by "seem," ought to come from the learner and not from the original text.

In addition to "seem," the modal "would" was also used by learners to express uncertainty (66):

(66)   With the congress, there will be a new Peruvian constitution. With the new type of government, there would be a better relationship with foreign countries. [113B]

In this excerpt, the learner wrote about the consequences of a new Peruvian congress. It interesting to note that to describe the first consequence, namely, a new constitution, the learner used the future tense, expressed by the modal "will." However, to describe the second consequence, she used the modal "would," which appears to encode both futurity and uncertainty. It is quite possible that the different degrees of certainty relative to both consequences can be explained by looking at the status of both ideas in the text. The first consequence is rather explicitly stated. The second is not, but it may be inferred from related information. Thus, it should not be surprising that the writer felt less sure of the truth of the second consequence.

Vague Language

Vague language was found in the recall protocols although not nearly to the extent that it was observed in the recall protocols of the Spanish newspaper text. For instance, there were no topic-only or existential-like sentences. Rather, the vague language in the English recall protocols referred overwhelmingly to topics which were unclear but about which a comment was made. This suggests that learners, not surprisingly, were somewhat more successful in constructing larger chunks of meaning during the reading of the L1 texts, than they had been while reading the L2 text.

There was apparently some confusion with regard to the proper names mentioned in each text, particularly the individual mentioned in the expository text, and the Peruvian village mentioned in the newspaper text. However, learners were able to cope with this confusion, at least to the extent that they were able to comment on these topics.

Learners used vague modifiers in order to compensate for missing or incomplete information. Consider the examples in (67- 69):

(67)   In some shanty town. [...] [126B]
(68)   Even in one xxxx village ^**Villa de** ^ **San ? Seville** where [...] [117B]
(69)   [...] proven by the man with the "still" camera . [104C]

In (67), by using "some," the writer marked the village under discussion as being specific, yet failed to provide the name, ostensibly because she was unable to do so. This analysis is supported by the reference to the same town in (68), where not only the use of "one" but also the signs of later editing indicate that the learner was initially unable to generate the name. In this case, the learner referred to the topic only vaguely as "one village," but at some later point, wrote "Villa de Seville" above the original writing. The learner further modified the correction, albeit with some hesitancy, as indicated through the interrogative mark, by inserting "San?." In (69), the learner did not attempt to give a name to the person, but modified "the man," such that it was clear who he was talking about.

In some cases, the learners simply left blanks for the missing information. Again, this was a limited phenomenon, found only in the case of two proper names, "Villa el Salvador" and "Eadweard Muybridge" (70-72):

(70)   In a small shanty town Villa d. _____, [...] [124B]
(71)   In the town of _____ la V   , known for [...] [204]B
(72)   Eadweard Muy - - - [...] [111C]

In these examples, the learners signaled the missing information by using blank spaces (71), underlines spaces (70-71) and even a series of dashes (72). This scaffolding is important because, like the vague modifier examples above, it provides an almost physical structure in which learners can express information. These lexically empty yet clearly marked spaces seem to indicate that the learners were aware that they had a problem being specific, and furthermore wanted to communicate that they at least knew that there was something else to be said.

In some cases, learners used what Channell (1994) refers to as "placeholders," expressions of vagueness such as "thing" and "something," in place of nouns. According to Channell, these placeholders are used when speakers can not or do not wish to use a more precise designation for the concept or item under consideration. While it is, of course, common for speakers to conceal certain information intentionally, it seems reasonable to suggest that expressions of vagueness in the recall protocols indicate an inability to be more precise.

This lack of precision may be the result of one of several conditions. For example, the learner truly might not have known (or could not remember) the correct expression at the time of writing. That possibility seems to be expressed in the following excerpt (73):

(73)   The two factors are [...] static motion and (something else) ^**stability**. [126C]

Similar to what was seen in (68), the subsequent editing of the excerpt in (73) suggests that the learner was initially unable to write a more exact proposition. Only after leaving a vague expression in its place was she able to recover what she believed to be the correct information. Hence, vague language is a strategy for the recovery of information.

Another possible source of the learner's inability to be specific may actually be due, not to a lack of information, but to the cognitive demands of the task. This possibility is raised by the following examples, which are notable for the prevalence of the expression "thing" throughout (74-76):

(74)   Static motion & dynamic motion involve 2 things. [115C]

(75)   Static balance is when a crawling thing [...] [117C]

(76)   There are two differences between things which are statistically [sic] balanced [...] and those which are dynamically balanced. Things which are statistically balanced [...] dynamically balanced things. [...] [106C]

It is revealing that examples such as these were only found in the recall protocols of the expository text, and as part of a discussion of two types of balance, arguably the most difficult section of the text. Additionally, it should be observed that in these examples, the word "thing" acts as a placeholder for relatively banal and general information (i.e. object, vehicle). In fact, the important and distinguishing information (i.e. static vs. dynamic things) is explicit in the recall, suggesting that "thing" was used, not as a placeholder for information that could not be recovered, but rather as a pronoun of a sorts, replacing "vehicle" or object." Thus, it could reasonably be argued that examples (73-76) do not constitute examples of "vague language" in the sense that the learner did not know what to say. Rather, the vague terms appear almost pronominal, used in a way similar to what has been seen with continued pronominalization and other ambiguous uses of pronominal reference. The following example provides further support for this proposal (77):

(77)   The idea of balance then is different for stationary things and things in motion. Stationary objects require constant balance whereas objects in motion [...] [120C]

Here, the learner began by writing about "things," but later referred more precisely to "objects." Again, the presumed "low semantic load" of a word like "object" makes it seem unlikely that the writer had encountered difficulty in recalling the word in the same sense that the learner in (73) was unable to generate "stability." Rather, the switch to "object" is probably an indication of a shift in control, which allowed the learner the cognitive distance necessary to focus in on such a detail. That is, her most immediate attention was not being directed elsewhere.

There were several examples of vague categories markers in the English recall protocols, two of which, involving the tag "etc.," are presented below (78-79):

(78)   [...] after ~~firing~~ ~~xxxx~~ banning the constitution, courts, other officials etc. [...] [119B]

(79)   [...] people didn't even think that ~~one's~~ a horse's hooves left the ground at a trot; men's feet, cheetah's paws etc. [sic] all display dynamic motion [...] [109C]

However, these examples appear not to correspond to ad hoc categories, which were shown to indicate uncertainty, but rather to common categories. In both excerpts, the learners were involved in making a list of a particular class of items, which appears almost well defined in the sense that they were able to give several examples. Thus, the tag "etc." did not act to create an ad hoc category, but rather to close a common one. Given the size of the classes in question, this step seems necessary if the learner was to be able to shift orientation and write about other aspects of the experimental text.

REFERENCE

As argued in the previous chapter, the way in which writers refer or fail to refer to topics in the discourse can be indicative of self-oriented language. Ambiguity, abbreviation, and, at times, redundancy were all characteristics of the English recall protocols, and suggest that the learners encountered difficulty constructing meaning from both texts. However, these features manifested themselves to varying extents and different degrees, both between the two English texts, and when compared to the Spanish recall protocols. Again, these differences suggest that the difficulties and the resulting private writing were distinct for each text.

Unmarked Shifts in Reference

Continued pronominalization despite shifts in topic can produce ambiguity for the reader although not for the writer, who does not need to distinguish topics and in fact does not always do so, presumably because her attention is needed elsewhere. The amount of ambiguity in the English recalls, especially as pertains to pronominal reference, was somewhat different than what was found in the protocols of the

Spanish text. For instance, there were few examples of continued pronominalization despite shifts in topic. This may be, in large part, due to the fact that, unlike
the Spanish newspaper article, the English texts had but one named character each.
Thus, for example, continued pronominal reference to Fujimori, as in the case of
the newspaper article, while frequent, was not a cause of ambiguity for the reader
simply because there was no other character to whom the writer might have
possibly referred.

   Unmarked shifts in references were found in some of the recalls of the English
newspaper text, but were limited to the discussion of a particular passage of the
newspaper article, where several groups of people were mentioned. Interestingly,
these groups were not referred to with pronouns per se, but rather with numerals
(i.e. "two") and quantifiers (i.e. "many"). Even so, such language is confusing for
the reader. Compare, then, the following examples (80):

(80)   Fujimori hopes the polls will be filled with people [...] Rebels have tried to inter-
       fere with polling. There have rocking throwing [sic] and small bombs set off.
       Two have been injured. No one has been killed. [106B]

   In this example (80) it is not clear who has been injured, the number "two" by
itself leaves open the possibility that either the people at the polling places or even
the rebels themselves were hurt.

   One protocol of the expository text contained several instances of ambiguity
(81):

(81)   Dynamics of walking so complex that not even computers can recreate the action
       through biofeedback. A few years ago, it was not known whether, in walking, all
       4 legs left the ground, but the stop action photography of Eadward [sic] Muy-
       bridge proved that it does, along w/ xxxx other creatures—the horse, the cheetah,
       etc. [108C]

The first ambiguity is related to the problem of the "4 legs" mentioned in the protocol. It is not clear from the recall alone whose legs the learner referred to,
although, it is likely that the reference came from the mention of a horse in the
original text. The antecedent of the second ambiguity, the underlined "it," is
somewhat harder to trace.

   The above example notwithstanding, most shifts in reference in the expository
text were clearly marked. Interestingly, there was one instance where the writer
apparently went back and corrected a potentially ambiguous use of the pronoun
"this" by later inserting "problem" afterwards (82):

(82)   The [sic] used to be some debate over whether or not horses had all of their feet
       off the ground at any point in their trot. This ^problem was solved with the
       development [...] [204C]

It is perhaps debatable whether the use of "this" by itself would have ever been read as ambiguous or not. However, this correction is especially revealing because it is evidence of an orientation toward making the text understandable to outsiders. Although the writer may have originally been engaged in private speech, at some point he was oriented toward making this speech socially comprehensible.

Abbreviation

Although ambiguous pronominal reference was limited, other forms of abbreviation were nonetheless quite common in the protocols. Consider the following examples (83-84):

(83)   New Congress will have 80 members [101B]
(84)   There are two types of balance: [...] The first is that.[...] Second is [...] [113C]

In both excerpts, what appears to be missing, from a communicative point of view, are the determiners preceding "New" (83) and "Second" (84). Additionally, in (84), the word "difference" has been left out of both the phrases "the first" and "second." This sort of abbreviation was more common in, although not limited to, the recalls of the expository text (85-87):

(85)   Reasons why walking hard to imitate. [101C]
(86)   Speed and momentum should be considered when talking about stability of object. Difference between dynamics and stable movements. Studies done to see if all 4 legs of a horse are up when he is trotting. They aren't. [119C]
(87)   Takes place in Lima, Peru. [...] Only two people had minor injuries, no deaths [...] Monday the results. [118B]

The language of these excerpts is telegraphic and reminiscent of notetaking. It is, in most cases, abbreviated, and, in some instances, resembles a list. In the recalls of the expository text, the orientation toward notetaking was even greater and, in several occasions, the recalls took on an outline form, as can be seen in the following example (88):

(88)   ^2 **major differences** between statically balanced and dynamically balanced ^**in a crawling system**
       1) definition of stability—in running a man's body provides the base of support for his walking legs
       2) consideration of speed and momentum
       depends on where the center of gravity is [end] [108C]

The expository text listed, discussed, and compared a number of differences between two types of balance. The learner in this last excerpt appears to have externalized information in such a way that it would facilitate the recall of additional information. By making a list and thus separating concepts, the learner was able to compare and contrast the appropriate information. Thus, this is private writing, not only because of its linguistic features, but also because of the way and where it has been externalized on the page.

Further examples of abbreviation include the following (89-90):

(89)   [...] Fujimori had won [...] Fuj. [sic] seized [...] Fuji's [sic] government. [103B]
(90)   Many machines imitate nature (ex. birds -> airplanes). [101C]

What is interesting about these examples is that they represent culturally acceptable forms of abbreviation. For instance, the abbreviation in these examples has not caused ambiguity, and moreover, they are known forms of semiotic mediation. In (89), the learner marked the abbreviated "Fuj." with a period, a social convention for marking abbreviations. Thus, the writer signaled her recognition that she produced a reduced, yet acceptable and transparent, form. For that reason, it seems reasonable to suggest that this type of abbreviation merits a different status in that it represents a more conscious, although no less strategic, orientation toward her production.

Focus and Externalization

The recall protocols of the newspaper text presented several examples of focus, in which full, unabbreviated forms continued to occur even though there were no shifts in reference (91-92):

(91)   The congress had been abolished 7 months earlier [...]The congress will have 80 members. [105B]
(92)   These elections, he says, will be interpreted as support for his actions if he wins a congressional majority. The elections will also reinstate Peru's credibility with foreign countries. [114B]

The retained forms in these excerpts suggest that the learners had focused on the underlined information, in an effort to generate more details regarding those items.

There were no instances of repeated externalization in the recall protocols of the expository text. That may be a result of the fact that, in the difficult section of the text, precisely what learners had to do was to go back and forth and compare two concepts. Thus, there was little opportunity for repeated mention of any one concept. What is further interesting is that the switches were clearly marked. Despite shifts in reference, there were no examples of continued pronominalization, because learners, categorically did not replace these concepts with pronouns (93-94):

(93)   <u>Static</u> + <u>Dynamic</u> balance are different: <u>Staticly</u> [sic] balanced vehicles are balanced if they have a tripod of support. <u>Dynamically</u> balanced vehicles can tip
over. [103C]

(94)   In order for a machine to walk or run, the <u>static</u> balance and the <u>dynamic</u> balance
must be considered [...] The first difference between <u>static</u> and <u>dynamic</u> motion
is the definition of stability. In <u>static</u> balance, the position of the balancing parts
of an object or animal are taken into account for a specific instant. In <u>dynamic</u>
balance the animal or object may be tipped at one time but is balanced over the
average of all the times [202C]

The closest the learners came to using pronouns was with vague language, as discussed earlier (95):

(95)   There are two differences between <u>things</u> which are statistically [sic] balanced
[...] and those which are dynamically balanced. <u>Things</u> which are statistically
balanced [...] dynamically balanced <u>things</u> [...] [106C]

In these examples (93-95), the distinguishing features "static" and "dynamic"
were never suppressed or replaced with pronouns, even when vague language (i.e.
"things") was present. This suggests that while some abbreviation was allowed,
there was in fact a minimum of information (namely, "static" and "dynamic') that
needed to be externalized at all times. One possible explanation is that this particular information was focus of the writers' mental activity, as they attempted to
define the two concepts. Such an explanation is consistent with the presence of
other private speech features (such as epistemic markers and vague language)
which provide evidence that the discussion of these two concepts was apparently
the most difficult of the text. An alternative explanation might be that the learners
had been socialized into dealing with expository texts in a particular way, namely,
they ought to be very explicit.

Mention of Text/author(s)

Finally, in several cases there were peculiar mentions of the author or text in the
middle of a protocol, without previous mention of either. Consider the following
examples (96-98):

(96)   On Nov. 22, there was a vote in Peru [...] although no results were known at the
time of the <u>article</u>. [203B]

(97)   ~~Since m~~Man has built machines that imitate ^**almost all** the actions of animals,
such as an airplane that flys [sic] like ^a bird, except walking and running. The
<u>author</u> ~~xxxx~~ tried to find [...] [104C]

(98)   This <u>article</u>, with all its sentences jumbled around dealt with balance and motion
and animals. The first <u>paragraph</u> [...] talked about the fact [....].
Eadweard Muybridge's device showed that animals, horses in particular did not

leave ground in a trot. ~~He~~ It said that other animals not only walk but also run (no shit) and use ballistic devices to help them do this [....].
A cruel thing to make students read. [203C]

The question is why the learners were not consistent in their reference to the text and author. One would expect the learners to mention them from the outset or not at all. If the writing were entirely private, as in the case of class or study notes, there ought to be no mention of the author or article. In the case of an entirely public recall, there might be clear and explicit references to the authors at the onset. Therefore, the mentions of the author and article which occur midway in the recall should be interpreted as indicative of the ongoing struggle between keeping something private and making something public. The writers' lack of control kept them from maintaining a consistent orientation, that is, what genre to use to summarize the experimental texts.

ON-LINE EDITING

On-line editing was a frequent characteristic of the recall protocols of the two English texts, and, as in the case of the Spanish recall, provided evidence of ongoing comprehension. Additionally, the English recall protocols present cases of the illusion of comprehension as well as what may be considered "the illusion of cohesion." The examples of on-line editing are important because they provide further evidence of the dynamic and fluid nature of generating a recall protocol. Namely, they show that, except for the most banal and brief of texts, writers of recall protocols are not involved in simply "recalling" cohesively stored information, but rather engage in the activity of (re)constructing meaning as they write.

On-going Comprehension

First, evidence of on-going comprehension is considered (99-102):

(99)   People in one ~~small~~ large shanty town [...] [101B]

(100)   There were 100,000 troops placed a voting centers to make sure that there was no ~~fraud or irregularities~~ ^**violence** in the election. 250 observers were placed to look for fraud and irregularities. [118B]

(101)   Strong support is shown for Alberto K. Fujimori* But it is unclear whether he has the parliamentary support he sought. *and his congress that will rewrite the Peruvian constitution. [110B]

(102)   Fujimori hopes the polls will be filled with people because ~~today's~~ high numbers of ~~people~~ will show ^**that** support for ~~Fujimori~~ him is strong and [...] [106B]

The above excerpts all contain evidence of on-line correction or editing which illustrates how learners revised or added to what they had written previously. In (99) and (100), the learners reversed their original statements. In (99), the learner replaced "small" with "large." Excerpt (100) is particularly interesting because it shows how the learner had initially confused the purpose of two groups involved in the elections. Originally, she wrote that the troops had been placed to guard against "fraud or irregularities." Next, she began to write about the purpose of the 250 observers, and at some point shortly thereafter realized that it was the observers and not the troops who were on the look out for fraud and irregularities. After completing that sentence, or perhaps even before, the learner went back, crossed out what she then knew to be incorrect, and inserted a more appropriate proposition. This example illustrates particularly well how writing is an act of constructing meaning with external semiotic tools which can then further facilitate comprehension.

In (101), the learner tried to provide additional information, extending the sentence to include what she has marked with an asterisk (*). The position of the addition relative to the original phrase is revealing, and suggests that the learner generated the extra information not long after writing the original statement. In (102), the writer reworked the sentence, almost entirely on-line, as indicated by the position of the added information, which is, in most cases, inserted after, rather than above the crossed-out information.

The Illusion of Comprehension

A further feature of the protocols, although not quite so robust as what has been found in previous research, is the "illusion of comprehension" (Appel & Lantolf, 1994). Appel and Lantolf have shown that readers often overestimate their comprehension of a passage, and only upon speaking about the text do they realize it. In the oral recall protocols of Appel and Lantolf's study this confrontation was often signaled by metacomments such as "I forgot" and a clear shift in orientation toward trying to figure out the text. In the written protocols, the illusion of comprehension is evident in editing and in apparent departures from the initial plan. Compare, for instance, the following excerpts (103-104):

(103)   The piece entitled "Machines that walk" addressed [sic] the problem. [...] [109C]
(104)   The newsarticle entitled about the quasi dictator [...] [109B]

These examples reveal the learner's orientation, in both cases, to the activity of reporting on the texts, part of which entailed providing a summary macrostructure mentioning the title of the text. In (103), writing about the expository text, the learner was successful. In (104), however, this same learner, writing about the newspaper text, reveals both her intention and inability to produce the title. The crossed out "entitled" shows that the learner originally intended to provide the name of article, presumably because she thought she could, and failed to realize that she could not until attempting to produce it. Because the writing of the recall protocols was not videotaped, it is not known whether the learner paused and tried to access the title or not before crossing out "entitled" and continuing with the protocol.

The following example, seen earlier, is particularly interesting because it illustrates both the illusion of comprehension as well as on-line comprehension (105):

(105)   The two factors that differ btwn. [sic] static motion and gravitational motion are
          speed and momentum and (something else) ^**stability**. [126C]

The excerpt begins with the learner's intention to name two factors, but when she attempted to write them both, she realized that she could not, and was forced to use vague language as a placeholder for the missing information. At some later point, however, she was able to generate the missing factor and inserted it in the appropriate spot. Particularly revealing is that the writer had originally wrapped the vague placeholder "something else" in parenthesis, as if to suggest that it was not part of the recall text. When she was able to fill in the missing factor, she crossed out both the vague language and the parenthesis, thus signaling that the new information indeed belonged to the text.

The following example illustrates a similar situation in which the learner originally thought she was going to be able to generate more information than she actually could (106):

(106)   Static + dynamic motion have two differences; first static
          [a space of about 2 inches]
          Machines must have both static and dynamic motion in order to walk [109C]

In this case, the learner was not able to access either of the differences that she originally claimed to have known. Unlike the previous example, however, this learner did not leave a lexical place holder for the missing information. Interestingly, though, she did leave a rather generous amount of space, about 2 inches, perhaps in the hope that she would be able to fill it at a later point. This, in fact, she failed to do.

In a final example, a learner crossed out a phrase which apparently was about to introduce more information (107):

(107)   The velocity of a dynamic object can affect its balance. For example, [end of
          protocol] [114 C]

However, because the scratched out "for example" was the last line in this particular protocol, it is impossible to know for certain why this learner did not continue.

It is possible that he realized that he could not give an example, but it is equally as plausible that at that point time ran out. For whatever reason, the writer knew that he could not continue and scratched out that portion of the recall which would have indicated that he was going to do so.

The Illusion of Cohesion

Another feature of the recall protocols which was made evident by the on-line editing is what may be called the "illusion of cohesion." In these cases, learners attempted to create a cohesive text and failed, and in a few instances, attempted to eliminate traces of this failure. Consider the following examples (108-110):

(108)   ~~Since m~~Man has built machines that imitate ^**almost** all the actions of animals, such as an airplane that flies like ^**a** bird, except walking and running. [104 C].

(109)   There was little violence during the election, despite guerrilla threats. Only 2 people were injured when dinamite [sic] was thrown at polling places. In addition, many peruvians [sic] turned out to vote even though several large groups expressed opposition to the endeavor. [109B].

(110)   Fujimori went to speak to citizens. After practically running a dictatorship, after ~~xxxx~~ banning constitution, courts, other officials, etc. He feels that April 5 campaign may have had a great influence on voting. [119B]

The above examples suggest that the learners originally intended to link together several clauses but were unable to do so. In (108), the sentence initial conjunction "since" implies that the learner at least initially had intended to produce a complex sentence. When he realized that he was unable to do so, he simply crossed out the conjunction, thus leaving an internally cohesive sentence.[7] In contrast, the learners whose excerpts are presented in (109-110) seemed not to have realized or have been concerned about the cohesion being attempting. In (109), the conjoining phrase "in addition" seems incongruous; it is not clear to which previous information this would be linked. In (110), it is not clear if the phrase headed by "after" was to be conjoined to the previous sentence or to the following one.

There is one example of the illusion of cohesion where a learner actually had to undertake quite a bit of editing in order to correct the failed cohesion. She was not able to repair the cohesion problem in the sense that she was not able to link information together at a higher level. Interestingly, however, she was able to cross out the language that suggested that she had attempted such cohesion, thus allowing her sentences to stand alone (111):

(111)   ^**Fujimori** ~~After~~ disbanding ^**ed** Congress, the cabinet, and suspending ^**ed** the Peruvian constitution on April 5, . ~~Fujimori w/this victory~~ [126B]

It appears that the learner originally tried to produce the phrase "After disbanding Congress, the cabinet and suspending the Peruvian constitution," and to follow it with the connected phrase which would have been headed by "Fujimori w/this victory." However, the learner was apparently unable to generate the information required in order to proceed. At that point, she stopped and modified the formal features of the original phrase, altering it so that it would not appear dependent on a proposition she was unable to produce. Thus, by working with what she had on the page already, inserting a subject and changing a few endings, the learner produced the internally cohesive and independent clause "Fujimori disbanded Congress, the cabinet and suspended the Peruvian constitution on April 5."

Even the failed attempts at cohesion are interesting because they provide evidence that some writers tried to produce cohesive texts but were unable to do so. This orientation was not prevalent in the Spanish recall protocols, probably because after reading the Spanish newspaper text, many learners had not understood enough to construct a cohesive discourse. Indeed, as remarked earlier, it would seem that they had enough trouble generating coherent statements, let alone linking them to one another. There were also few examples of cohesion, failed or otherwise, in the expository text. That may be because this text was also too difficult, for other reasons, to allow the learners to attempt cohesion.

SUMMARY

The recall protocols of the English texts revealed signs of private writing, albeit less than what was found in the Spanish recall protocols. Nevertheless, the private writing indicated hesitancy and difficulty. It also suggested that even the task of recalling texts read in one's native language was challenging enough that learners had to avail themselves of the problem-solving strategies of externalized cognition. This is not surprising; Kintsch (1977) maintains that even native speakers generally are only able to recall between 10 percent and 25 percent of narrative texts. What is of interest here, however, is how learners express and cope with this difficulty through the use of their cognitive tool: linguistic mediation.

The private speech features provided information about the learners on-going mental activity. Private speech was realized somewhat differently for all three sets of protocols, which indicates that, in general, the three texts (differing in language and content) provoked different activity on the part of some writers. Reading and recalling each experimental text was difficult, but in distinct ways, and the private speech indicated that learners reacted to various types and degrees of difficulty in different ways. For the Spanish text, as was said earlier, most learners were only able to piece together fragments of the original text, that is, words that they recognized or could figure out. They were probably not able to parse entire sentences from the text.

For the English newspaper text, the learners did seem to understand—at least at a local level—most of what was going on in the text, as indicated by the amount of detail and elaboration. However, they were often unable to construct cohesive narratives, revealing that at a global level, their comprehension was less than complete. In the case of the expository text, learners also appeared to have understood much of the local level propositional content of the text, some passages better than others. There was evidence that the difficulty lay in keeping the facts straight: in describing, comparing, and contrasting the factors involved in the two types of balance discussed. The problem was not constructing a cohesive narrative, since it was not a narrative text. Rather, it was in constructing a complete and coherent recall. In some cases, the learners appeared to be engaged instead in the activity of writing notes or in an attempt at reconstructing the content of the text, as shown by abbreviation phenomena.

Finally, there was evidence that orientation differed individually between learners and changed within learners. For example, some students were oriented toward reporting, others to retelling. Also, it was shown that orientation sometimes changed during the course of the recall activity. Both of these issues will be taken up in greater detail in the following chapter.

NOTES

[1]   Again, the learners" number are given in brackets. Learners [101-127] are third semester, elementary students, [201- 205] are fifth semester, intermediate learners. The letter refers to the text: A = the Spanish newspaper text, B = the English newspaper text, C = the English expository text.

[2]   Why this learner may have been so oriented will be discussed in the following chapter.

[3]   Most of the protocols which began by discussing balance did so in the context of a summary macrostructure. This suggests that the learners were conscious of the fact that they were summarizing the text, and in doing so changing the order of presentation, which they marked by writing "this article discusses" and the like.

[4]   Personal history, including one's academic experience, is a factor in determining orientation.

[5]   While these learners did not use the past to describe the "on-going" elections, they did, of course, use the past to talk about certain background events and other completed actions, as did the original text itself.

[6]   The learners' orientation to specific lexical items, including "statistical" and static," will be taken up in the following chapter.

[7]   This example is also especially interesting because the unrealized conjunction was sentence initial, as opposed to sentence internal. Thus, there was actually some (i.e. temporal, cognitive, physical) distance between the conjunction and what would have been the second clause. Perhaps it is the case that the orientation toward conjoining sentences could not be maintained for that length of time, that is, the learner forgot (or was unable to maintain focus on) what he wanted to conjoin.

5

Synthesis: Private Writing, Orientation and Activity

This chapter attempts to summarize and further illustrate some of the more striking features of orientation made evident by the recall protocol data. Orientation, as discussed in Chapter 2, is a central although often overlooked feature of human activity. It refers to the way in which people view a given task and how they deploy strategies in order to engage the task in light of the potential difficulties that the task may present. The way in which an individual orients herself to a given task is based on her goals, her continued assessment of the problem and her ongoing progress in the activity. The individual's orientation and subsequent activity is a product of her immediate perception of the situation and sociocultural history.

As has been argued throughout, Sociocultural Theory maintains that language has two macro-functions: a social function and a private function. Thus, the writing in the protocols in this study may minimally reflect the communicative function of relating the content of the experimental texts, or the cognitive function of trying to discover or (re)construct meaning through writing. What will become evident in the data to be presented shortly is that these two orientations are not mutually exclusive. Thus, it is possible—and indeed often the case—that both orientations are realized as learners struggle to make enough sense of the text to be able to relate it in a coherent manner. Sometimes, however, there is a clear, albeit tenuous, balance in favor of one of the two orientations, which may fluctuate during the course of the activity. This fluctuation reflects the learners' ongoing struggle to be social in the midst of a difficult and supposedly communicative task and is by far the most defining characteristic of the recalls.

This chapter looks more closely at the linguistic realizations of orientation and shifts in orientation in order to understand the learners' activity in the task, and to discover properties of orientation and activity in general. Specifically, the discussion will focus on discovering how private and public orientations are realized throughout the protocols. The data presented in the following sections will reveal that orientation is not stable across individuals, nor within the same individual, even for the same task. Thus, learners approached the task of producing a recall, each with a distinct orientation, converting the task into different activity. It will also be shown that, when faced with sufficient difficulty, some writers modified their activity significantly.

The following section presents examples of the learners' initial orientation to the task of producing a recall protocol, paying special attention to differences in orientation across learners. In the second section, we see how orientation shifts, both definitively and temporarily in the middle of the task. The third section presents data that illustrates the learners' orientation to the actual page on which the protocols were written, and discusses what this can tell us about the learners' orientation to the task. The fourth section considers the lexical properties of the recall protocols and their contribution to our understanding of the learners' orientation.

ORIENTATION AT THE OUTSET OF RECALL

In this section, we consider the learners' initial orientation to the task of producing a recall protocol. That is, the orientation adopted by the learners at the outset of writing, as evidenced through their initial written comments, macrostructures and the like, which will be taken as indicative of their intentions. For the sake of argument it is assumed that at the outset all of the learners understood that the task implied producing a "social text," that is, a recall that would be later read by the experimenter. However, what is of interest is whether or not such a strictly social orientation could be maintained at the time of writing.

As was documented in Chapters 3 and 4, and will be brought to light again here, the recall protocols exhibited several different orientations, which were largely made evident by the ways in which learners initiated the recalls. For the most part, many learners appeared to be predominantly, if not entirely, oriented toward the social or reader-directed task of relating the content of the experimental texts. The learners' introductory comments reflect their social intention, although, in some instances, the private writing betrays a co-existing orientation to the self. In a few cases, however, the initial writing reflects a decidedly more self-oriented slant, suggesting that even at the commencement of writing, the learners were more involved in understanding the text so that recall could become possible.

Initial Orientation to Reader

In the majority of the recalls it is clear that the learners were, at least initially, predominantly oriented toward the other-directed activity of relating the content of the experimental texts. This social orientation was often realized in one of two ways: as either "reproducing" or "reporting on" the original text. Reproducing the original text often, but not always, included the attempted recreation of the discursive features of the original texts, such as a title, or, in the case of the newspaper texts, a dateline, as well as the reconstruction of the propositional content of the text. The reporting strategy was often characterized by the presence of a summary macrostructure and reference to the article or author, and a more distanced presentation of the propositional content of the text.

These strategies appear consistent with the socially oriented goal of reconstructing and relating the experimental text, and there is nothing to suggest that they are not appropriate ways of initiating text recall for learners who have more or less understood what they have read and wish to convey that information to a reader. That is, there is nothing inherent to either "reporting" or "reproducing" that suggests that the learner was struggling for control. In fact, they seem to suggest quite the opposite—an orientation to be "public."

That notwithstanding, there is evidence to suggest that some learners encountered problems attempting to establish a strictly public orientation. For example, incomplete, unfinished, or edited macrostructures and titles indicate that the orientation undertaken (e.g. toward reporting on or reproducing the original text) was, in fact, too difficult for learners who had not understood the text in the first place. Compare, for instance, the macrostructures in (1) and (2):

(1)   Machines that walk deals with the two major differences between static and dynamic balance machines. [118C].
(2)   Motion is discussed as being ~~xxxx~~ able to be copied mechanically and then different types of locomotion—walking, opposed to running. [205C].

Both macrostructures indicate an orientation on the part of the writers toward relating the content of the text. However, the macrostructure in (2) reveals evidence of a simultaneous orientation to the self as well. While the learner initially appeared to be reporting on the text, in the content of a single sentence he later shifted into an abbreviated (i.e. verbless) and less coherent discursive style that is suggestive of an orientation toward knowing rather than relating. The protocols present abundant examples along these lines, which suggests that learners were often manifesting both self- and other-orientation at the start of writing.

It bears repeating that of the two above-mentioned strategies used to implement an initially social orientation, there were slightly more instances of summary macrostructures in the recalls of the L1 expository text. Furthermore, reference to an author or authors was limited to only those recalls. As suggested in Chapter 4, it seems plausible that this is a vestige of the learners' orientation to scientific or academic texts.

Initial Orientation to Self

Although many of the learners appeared to be initially oriented to the reproducing or reporting on the experimental texts, there were instances in which the learners' opening remarks were indicative of more self-oriented writing. This is the case of opening strategies such as producing a narrative, and planning the recall by initially writing down an outline or other information. Unlike the strategies reported earlier (reproducing and reporting), these initial strategies do seem to suggest an inherently private or problem-solving orientation for this task. This finding is further supported by the linguistic properties through which these strategies are deployed. Thus, even from the beginning a few learners were predominantly oriented toward and engaged in the activity of problem solving.

There were several examples in which learners apparently first copied down bits of information before writing the main text of the protocol. In most cases, this information consisted of names, numbers, and dates. For example, one learner wrote the following, before starting the recall "text" (3):

(3)   (287,000 million) (23, Friday) [110A]

That this was written first is suggested by its position in the middle of the recall text, which continues above and below the information in (3). The recall contains an arrow that directs the reader (or perhaps even the writer) to its continuation below. The position of the information in (3), and the fact that the learner wrote around it suggests that the learner wrote this information first in order to remember it, perhaps with the intention of later incorporating it into the recall.

In a similar example, one learner [104B] wrote down "Villa de Salvador" in the uppermost part of page, below which was written the recall. However, in the body of the text, the village is left unnamed and instead is referred to as "one of the smallest ^shabbiest towns." This suggests that the learner copied down the name of the town at the outset in order to remember it. Unfortunately, when he got to the relevant point in his recall, he seemingly forgot that he had the name of the town available. This may have been due to the difficulty being encountered as he attempted to produce a coherent recall of the text. Perhaps, since he had shifted orientation from self- to other-, the learner was operating in a different discursive space.

These examples are important because they indicate that some of the learners' initial written production had an undeniably private function. Namely, they were oriented toward knowing and remembering certain information, in order to facilitate the primary activity (or the activity associated with the overriding goal) of relating that information as part of a coherent recall text.

Learner [104] apparently availed himself of this pre-recall writing strategy for more than just retaining certain information. Instead, he used this option to plan the subsequent recall of the English expository text. Consider the excerpt in (4), which appeared in the uppermost margin of the page, in significantly smaller writing, above a recall text of one paragraph:

(4)   imitation

     horse, man w/camera
     comparison dynamic & static (crawling/tripod
     [104C]

The items in the above list correspond to the organization and main topics of the experimental text. Furthermore the list reflects the organization of the protocol, presented below in (5), with the exception of the last item, which was not mentioned in the recall:

(5)   ~~Since m~~Man has built machines that imitate ^**almost all** the actions of animals, such as an airplane that flys [sic] like ^**a** bird, except walking and running. The author tried to find if this were possible through the use of computers. He also used the fact that while running humans and other animals leave the ground for a period of time, and even when a horse trots it does the same thing, proven by the man with a "still" camera. [104C]

The contents of the list, its relationship to the original text, and even its bullet-like structure, all distinguish it as an outline. Thus, the learner not only externalized the relevant information, but he also ordered it in such as way as to plan the subsequent writing of the recall text. His initial orientation, then, was to prepare for the writing of the recall. Clearly, these pre-recall planning remarks, both the outline and the other examples, are not meant for the reader. Rather, they are directed at the writers and represent their attempts at using language to mediate the cognitive processes necessary for recall.

It was observed in the preceding two chapters that there were several instances in the protocols where learners began their recalls of either of the two newspaper texts in a narrative or story-like, fashion, as evidenced by certain formulaic opening statements, and the use of the atemporal or historical present. This seems to belie an orientation toward retelling the newspaper reports as stories and as such reveals an underlying and indeed prevailing, orientation to the self. Clearly, there exists at some level an orientation to relate the content of the experimental texts.

However, the use of a narrative schema is clearly strategic and facilitating in nature, in that it allows the writers to focus their attention on the propositional content of the events, rather than on the way in which they were ordered (cf. Rumelhart, 1980 and articles therein). Thus, by beginning the recall of a newspaper text as if it were a personal narrative, the learner reveals a compelling orientation to the self, in the context of a seemingly other-oriented activity.

Assessment and Orientation: Memorization

There is one instance where the language of the recall protocol reveals not only the orientation of the learner at the time he initiated writing, but also seems to suggest a particular orientation to the task held at the time of reading. It will be suggested that the learner's actions at the time of reading the first experimental text were apparently directed at the production, memorization, and subsequent externalization of a word-for-word translation of the original text. However, this mnemonic orientation changed over the course of reading the three experimental texts. Consider his recall of the Spanish newspaper text, presented in its entirety below (6), and compare it with the first paragraph of the original text, given in (7) along with its translation:

(6) Miami United States of America 28th. President George Bush on Friday the 23rd passed the controversial law known as the Torricelli Law on the last days of his electoral campaign ^**in order** to maintain _____ over the Cuban community. [106A]

(7) Miami, EEUU. 28 octubre. El presidente de Estados Unidos, George Bush, firmó el viernes 23 en Miami la controvertida Acta para la Democracia en Cuba, conocida como ley Torricelli. Bush transformó la firma de la ley en unos de los últimos actos de su campaña electoral en Florida, en un intento por mantener a su lado a la comunidad de origen cubano. [TextA]

Miami, US. October 28th. The President of the United States, George Bush, signed, Friday the 23, in Miami, the controversial Act for Democracy in Cuba, known as the Torricelli law. Bush transformed the signing of the law into one of the last acts of his electoral campaign in Florida in an attempt to keep on his side the community of Cuban origin.

The similarities between the protocol and the first paragraph of the original text are striking. Some details are absent in the protocol, for example, the official name of the Torricelli law ("Act for Democracy in Cuba"). Also, there are few minor discrepancies between the two texts, for example, the learner wrote "passed" instead of "signed," "days" instead of "acts." Nonetheless, the two texts are very close, which shows that the writer was engaged in the activity of producing a literal translation of the first part of the text. This analysis appears to be supported by the underlined blank space in the last line of the protocol. Since the learner was writing in his native language, it seems likely that the lexical gap was rooted in the language of the original text, or more precisely perhaps, a specific word (*mantener* "to maintain") that he was not able to translate.

If this learner had indeed been oriented toward memorizing a translation of the text, the question that arises is why would he adopt such a seemingly difficult if not impossible to complete definition of the task? In order to answer this question, it is crucial to take the following information into consideration: This particular learner, after the administration of the first of the three experimental texts, indicated to the researcher that he had misunderstood the directions and had, he felt, made a mistake in completing the recall task. Specifically, the learner had read and written about only the first of the three paragraphs that made up the Spanish newspaper text.[1]

If this is true, then it is not surprising that this learner's orientation could be substantially different than that of the other 30 learners. After all, orientation is based in large part on a person's assessment of the situation and, in all likelihood, this learner's assessment of the situation was very different from someone who thought (correctly) that she had been asked to read and recall a much longer text. Thus, it seems plausible that the orientation toward memorization was made feasible based on having to read only one short paragraph.

What is interesting, however, is that this learner appears to have approached the recall of the second experimental text (the English expository text) with the same mnemonic orientation, even though he knew that it entailed reading a seemingly much longer text. Consider the following protocol, presented in its entirety (8).

(8)   Many machines imitate nature. The airplane imitates the soaring bird could machines ever learn to walk as humans.
      Research has shown that a horse does have all four of its legs off the ground at the same time. Muybridge showed this with still photography.
         There are two differences between things which are statistically [sic] balanced and those which are dynamically balanced. Things which are statistically balanced must be set as a tripod to remain stable. Dynamically balanced things are allowed to tip ever so slightly.
         There is another difference. [106C]

Compare the first paragraph of the recall protocol in (8) with that of the original text, given below (9):

(9)   Many machines imitate nature; a familiar example is the imitation of a soaring bird by the airplane. One form of animal locomotion that has resisted imitation is walking. Can it be that modern computers and feedback control systems make it possible to build machines that walk? We have been exploring the question with computer models and actual hardware. [Text C]

What is noteworthy about (8) is the apparent question in the first paragraph, which suggests that the learner was oriented toward memorization for this protocol as well. As noted earlier, this question is identifiable as such, not by an interrogative mark, but rather only by subject-verb inversion, and is furthermore neither answered nor made to fit cohesively into the surrounding discourse. Thus, it is plausible that the learner was again simply oriented toward copying down the text verbatim, focusing not on the meaning but on the words of the text. This time, however, he was successful only in copying down the first few lines of each paragraph of the original text. This is understandable, given that this text was considerably longer than the first text (which was, for this learner, only the first paragraph of the Spanish newspaper text.) Perhaps the lack of success accounts for his failure to carry his mnemonic orientation to the third text he was asked to read and recall. Compare his recall of the English newspaper text (10) with the original (11):

(10)   Lima Peru Nov 22 Elections are being held for the ^**new** congress of Peru, a congress which had been disbanded seven months ago ^**April 5th** along with its constitution by Fujimori who seized power. [106B]

(11)   LIMA, Peru. Nov 22. Surveys of voters leaving polling places today showed strong backing for Alberto K. Fujimori's candidates for a Congress that will rewrite the Peruvian constitution. But it was unclear whether Mr. Fujimori had won the parliamentary majority he had sought. [Text B]

A quick glance is enough to determine that the learner had not attempted to memorize the English newspaper text at all.[2] Although he did reproduce verbatim the dateline of the original text, there is no longer the direct correspondence between the original text and the recall that was observed for the other two texts.

The three protocols of this learner are especially interesting because they clearly illustrate the complex relationship between assessment, previous experience, orientation and even learning within the context of the experimental task. Based, although perhaps not entirely, on his perception that the experimental text was shorter than it actually was, the learner oriented himself toward memorizing and reproducing what he had read.[3] It seems reasonable to suggest that the relative success of his orientation led him to adopt it for the recall of a second and much longer text. In the same way, the subsequent failure of this approach probably accounted for its discontinuation by the third recall.

An Orientation Towards Complaining

The protocol of one learner revealed an orientation to complaining about the experimental text. This is an especially interesting protocol because it provides further evidence that learners reacted differently to the difficulty of the text and yields insight as to what might have gone on during the reading of text by this particular learner. The protocol is presented in its entirety below (12):

(12)   This article, with all its sentences jumbled around dealt with balance and motion and animals. The first paragraph seemingly intact, talked about the fact that machines that walk or run have not been developed and that people are looking to computer models to help discuss if this is possible.

   Eadweard Muybridge's device showed that animals, horses in particular did not leave ground ~~xxxx~~ in a trot. ~~He~~ ^**It** said that other animals not only walk but run (no shit) and use ballistic devices to help them do this.

——— THE INTERIM WAS VERY DISCOMBOBULATED [sic] ———

Then ——- In order to understand walking and running, remember to keep balance in mind.

   [arrow pointing to previous sentence]

   I think this was the last sentence

   [space of about 3 inches]

   A cruel thing to make students read. [203C]

The recall begins with a summary macrostructure, which, although somewhat general, is suggestive of an initial orientation to relate the content of the original text. However, the content and organization indicate that he was more specifically oriented toward relating the contents of individual sections of the text. Note, for example, the reference to the first paragraph, to an "interim" and to the "last sentence." Moreover, the learner uses bullets or dash marks and the word "then" to mark the divisions in the text. Those divisions notwithstanding, the learner is only able to relate information from some of the sections (or paragraphs) of the original text. Namely, he is able to summarize information for the first two paragraphs, and for the last section he is able to provide a few unconnected sentences. Thus, it can be said that this learner understood little more than the gist of the text. He apparently understood the opening remarks, but failed to penetrate the more technical part of the article to any degree.

   The propositional content aside, the most salient feature of the recall, however, is the writer's clear orientation to criticize and complain about the experimental text, and perhaps the experiment in general. What is particularly interesting is that the learner directs his critical and at times sarcastic comments at the text as a whole (which he deemed "cruel") as was well as toward specific sections therein (such the technical discussion, which he deemed "discombobulated"). No other learner presented such an orientation and, interestingly, this same learner did not criticize the other two experimental texts, which he was able to recall without much difficulty. Given the limited content of the recall, the most plausible explanation for this behavior is that the learner's criticism of the text is a realization of his orientation (or need) to blame the text itself for his failure to construct a significant amount of meaning.

It is very likely that the learner initially approached the reading of the text with an orientation to read and recall, much as he did the previous text (the Spanish newspaper article). The content of the recall suggests that he did understand the gist of the first couple of paragraphs of the original text. However, he clearly found the technical discussion incomprehensible, an assessment that evidently altered his orientation to the extent that he probably stopped trying to understand the text. Rather, his orientation had shifted to that of complaining or criticizing this "poorly written" text. In fact, this orientation was apparently so strong that when it came time to produce the written recall, his intention to denounce the text came through even as he related information he was able to understand (e.g. "no shit"). Moreover, the relative lack of evidence of on-going comprehension in the recall indicates that the writer was in no way oriented toward trying to understand the text any further, as other learners were shown to do.

In short, this recall is particularly revealing because it shows us how one learner reacted to the difficulty presented by the experimental text. Namely, he abandoned his assumed initial goal of trying to comprehend the text (something he did not do for the other two texts). Furthermore, at the time of writing the recall, he attempted to justify this decision by objecting to the text. What is perhaps more interesting is that the learner was the only one who reacted in this way, even though his assessment of the text was likely not unique. It may have been the case that the other learners simply did not believe that attacking the text or the task was an option. This may be true given that the experiment was situated in an academic setting, which is an activity space that normally does not allow students the freedom to lodge complaints about such matters.

SHIFTS IN ORIENTATION AND CHANGES IN ACTIVITY

We have seen, then, that the manifestations of orientation, as found in the private writing features of the protocols, reflect the ongoing struggle between being social and being private. Thus, the learners' initial behavior is often both self- and reader-directed, although in some cases it is possible to determine a more dominant orientation. We now consider evidence that orientation can shift during the writing of the protocol, as learners struggled to maintain a social orientation in the middle of a cognitively challenging activity. At times, the learners appear to have moved closer to a more exclusively social orientation, at others, they seem to be locked into a private orientation by the demands of the task. Sometimes these shifts are only temporary, as learners set and met subgoals associated with the activity of recalling the text. Other shifts appear to be more decisive, involving an almost irreversible shift in the self-reader balance, as learner redefined their goals (i.e. from "to relate" to "to understand," or something similar) and fundamentally altered their activity, in order to continue to engage in the task.

Decisive Shifts in Orientation and Activity

Many learners began writing the recall protocols oriented toward both the reader and the self, where one of these two orientations, usually the social, was predominant. The data show, however, that at times there was a marked and significant shift in the balance of control, as learners discovered that they could not complete the task of recalling a text that they had not understood. Some learners shifted their orientation to trying to figure out the text by writing about it, a shift in activity that did not always lead to success. Other learners, however, substantially altered their orientation, in such a way that their activity, although successful, bore little resemblance to the prescribed task of recalling the experimental texts.

The majority of the learners began writing with a predominantly social orientation. Consequently, most of the decisive shifts in orientation were in the direction of increasingly more private speech, as it became progressively more difficult to maintain control in the task of producing a recall. For most, the increase in self-oriented writing suggests that for these learners the activity had changed fundamentally. Thus, they were no longer engaged in trying to reconstruct the experimental text, rather they were trying to construct it by writing about it. Therefore, their written production represents not a retelling but actually a working out in writing of the content of the original text.

A proliferation of private speech features seems to be a clear indicator that learners had become oriented toward trying to comprehend the text. The most salient of these features is strategically external semiotic mediation, because it shows that writer not only failed to relate the text but actively used the language of the recall in an attempt to create meaning. Examples of externalization and other strategic private writing features, such as vague language and patterns of tense and aspect, were frequently observed in the recall protocols, as has been amply demonstrated in the previous two chapters. The following excerpt, seen earlier, is a particularly illustrative example of both externalization and vague language (13):

(13)   The law called Rotticelli [sic] law was recently passed by Bush in October ^(Fri-
       day 23rd) with the support of Robert Roticelli [sic] from New Jersey. It is a very
       controversial law It-and will some guy from Florida.
       It will get rid of the trade embargo between Cuba and the United States. It will
       get rid of the taxes also. This was worked out with Castro. This is all being done
       in the hope to establish democracy in Cuba. [107A]

The learner is not involved in simply relating information about the law in question. Rather, she is primarily involved in generating the relevant details by writing about it, or more specifically, by focusing on the bill via her external linguistic tools, a move which allows her to bring forth more information about the bill.

Externalization was prevalent in the recalls, as was vague language, which was argued to be strategically employed by learners in order to construct their recalls, despite gaps in knowledge. Abbreviation relieved learners of some of their cognitive load by allowing them to focus on the activity of reconstructing information. This strategy often resembled notetaking as learners struggled to piece together the text, a strategy that apparently reached its peak in the recall of one learner, whose protocol is presented below in its entirety (14):

(14) Dynamics of walking so complex that not even computers can recreate the action through biofeedback. A few years ago, it was not known whether, in walking, all 4 legs left the grown [sic] but ^**the** stop-action photographs of Eadward Muybridge proved that it does, along w/ ~~xxxx~~ other creatures - the horse, the cheetah etc.
       ^**2 major differences** between statically balanced & dynamically balanced—
       ^**in a** crawling system
       1) definition of stability—in running a man's body provides the base for his walking legs
       2) consideration of speed & momentum depends on where the center of gravity is [end] [108C]

As discussed earlier, the private writing features in this protocol, such as the abbreviated (i.e. verbless) macrostructure and the odd use of reference (i.e. the missing antecedent of "4 legs," "it") provide evidence that this learners had trouble producing the recall, ostensibly because she had not been able to comprehend the text at more than a superficial level. Thus, for her, the activity took on an orientation toward knowing rather than relating the original text. The orientation toward comprehending the text ultimately manifests itself in the writing of an outline in the second half of the protocol. In order to facilitate her comprehension of the technical part of the text, a comparison of two types of balance, the learner began to construct meaning in the form of an outline. This outline is an externalized and graphic representation of the dichotomy that the learner wanted to relate.

The production of an outline is particularly revealing of this learner's orientation to the task. She was so self-oriented and controlled by the text itself that she was unable to maintain a social orientation. Thus, her shift in activity from relating to comprehending occurred early on. By producing an outline, the learner fundamentally changed the discursive structure and even the genre of the recall text such that it no longer even looked like a social text, as one might have been able to say about the protocol in (13).

Another learner's shift to a cognitive orientation early on nonetheless had an almost communicative appearance (15):

(15) Is the walk of humans like other animals like the horse where at any given moment all its hoofs [sic] are off the ground. Yes, this in fact is true for humans as well. And how about dynamic stability versus static stability? A car must have 3 of its 4 tires on the ground to maintain stability, and so the humans must also have their feet tipped to maintain stability. [107 C]

Here, the learner's working out of the text takes the form of a continued dialogue with herself. The sequence of questions and answers lends a social cast to her private speech. While this particular format may have been primed by the appearance of a rhetorical question in the experimental text, the writer's generalization of the dialogue to other contexts suggests that it was also strategic in nature. Thus, the learner treated herself as a hypothetical or symbolical other with whom she could discuss and therefore come to know the content of the experimental text. Again, this seems to illustrate Vygotsky's claim that writing can be a "conversation with a white piece of paper" (John-Steiner 1985b, p.348).

In the following protocol, the learner shifted from one problem-solving orientation to another (16):

(16)   This is about George Bush, the president of the United States on Friday the 23rd, talking about the policy toward Cubans. He wants to place an embargo on the cubans [sic]. The leader of Cuba is Fidel Castro. This takes place in Florida. Bush wants Cuba to become a democracy. Bush spend [sic] 247.000 million dollars on something dealing with defense. 600 city dwellers were mentioned in this. A legislator from the state of Florida with the last name of Graham. This is a controvertial [sic] act that Bush wants to pass. Some don't agree with how he ~~xxxx~~ proposes to deal with it. Toricelli [sic] [end] [118A]

The learner introduced the recall with a story-like summary macrostructure, and began to relate the events in the atemporal present, suggesting that at least initially, she was oriented to retelling the text as a story. The first two lines of the recall are detailed and cohesive, indicating a degree of control in the task of relating the information. Nonetheless, as was argued previously, the use of a narrative schema is clearly strategic and therefore equally problem-solving in nature. Thus, the learner began the task of producing a recall protocol precariously balanced between private and social orientations. After the first two lines, however, the recall becomes increasingly more abbreviated, and even ambiguous ("This takes place in Florida") until, at one point, the learner failed to write a complete sentence ("A legislator from Florida with the last name of Graham.") The remaining text lacks cohesion; the individual sentences no longer clearly relate to each other, rather they appear to be a series of unconnected remarks that are primarily descriptive. Some of the information is from the learner's world knowledge (i.e. "The leader of Cuba is Fidel Castro"). The learner shifted, then, from recalling the text in a cohesive, albeit story-like manner, to simply listing or externalizing whatever information she was able to generate about the text, even drawing on world knowledge to complete the recall. Thus, the learner's writing activity became increasingly more self-oriented, a response which can presumably be attributed to the difficulties she encountered while trying to recall the text cohesively.

The learner whose protocol is given in (17) shows a similar pattern of shift in orientation:

(17) It was the 28th of October, a Friday. George Bush wants to have a compact or something of that sort for the Democracy of Cuba. He also wants the 3rd world countries not to deal w/ Fidel Castro [sic]. The representative of N.J. and Senator of Florida were not invited. Canada, France and Mexico opposed his ideas. Bush needs support. He wants that all of Cuba will be united under liberty.

600 citizens?
Torricelli - N.J. Senator? [125A]

The entire text of the recall is filled with private writing features, above all vagueness, and the sentences are brief and unconnected. Essentially, like the learner in (16), she provided a series of unrelated information, and ultimately, concluded the recall with a brief list of short items. Thus, the learner altered her activity definitively and in so doing converted it into one that she was able to sustain, albeit briefly. She abandoned the goal of producing a coherent discourse and instead contented herself with writing down the remaining information she was able to generate as a list. It is worth mentioning that whatever control she might have gained by this redefinition of the task appears to be mitigated by her doubts as to the accuracy of the information, which is expressed by interrogative marks.

We have seen then, that some learners shifted their orientation in the task of recall from that of recall to comprehension through writing. Some learners, like the ones above (16-17), abandoned the goal of writing a cohesive recall text, and simply listed information they thought to be true. These shifts in orientation in the recall task occurred as learners discovered that they were unable sustain their initial orientations. Thus, they sought success—control—in other, though related, activities. For some learners, however, control in the task was achieved only when the goal of the activity (and thus the activity itself) was changed more dramatically to one they were better able to achieve. These learners abandoned the seemingly unattainable goal of trying to the work out the text in writing, and opted, rather, to write about something they did understand, for example, extra-textual knowledge related to the facts of the text. Consider, then, the following recall of the Spanish newspaper text, given in its entirety (18):

(18) Oct 28. Bush signs law—The Torricelli Law. Senator Bob Graham ^**Florida** & Toricelli [sic] both are supporters of the law. The law is for the democracy of Cuba. Bush is visiting Miami on his electoral campaign. Bush gives a speech to the Miamians about how the U.S. will continue to fight the regime of Fidel Castro, will continue to work against the Communists of Cuba so that Miamians will once again be reunited w/their families in their homeland. <u>Bush is against the Communists of Cuba & the U.S. has in the past pursued</u> [end] [108A]

This is a particularly rich example because it allows us to see how this learner shifted orientations several times. The reproduction of the dateline indicated that she was initially oriented toward recalling the text. However, the repeated focus on the law and, subsequently, on Bush, implies that she had shifted her activity to trying to comprehend the text through writing. Finally, she ended the recall (underlined portion) by providing information that came not from the text itself but instead from her own general knowledge about US-Cuban affairs. It is at this point, then, that the focus disappears and the use of tenses becomes more appropriate from a communicative perspective. Thus, by changing her goal, literally to "write about something you know," the learner was able to gain control and relate information in way that suggested regulation in a social activity.

This final shift in orientation to a different, yet feasible, goal was characteristic of several other protocols, including two recalls of the expository text, the first of which is presented below in its entirety (19):

(19)   Walking is a motion that has resisted imitation. Speed and momentum should be considered when talking about stability of objects
Difference between dynamic and stable movements. Studies done to see if all 4 legs of a horse are up when he is trotting. They aren't. For a car to remain balanced during stability it must be on "on a tripod". For dynamic it can be on 2 wheels. When a person is running one leg goes up, then goes down. [119C]

The first paragraph is brief and not very cohesive, yet the real difficulties surface in the second paragraph where the writing turns into a list of abbreviated and unconnected sentences, as the learner tried to externalize what she could about the text. At some point, she apparently gave up, and stopped trying to comprehend the confusing technical discussion of the expository text. Instead, she wrote something that she knew about human motion in general, which was information so obvious that it was never stated in the text in the first place.

In the following example, the learner appeared to end the protocol with a bit of extratextual information that was seemingly not related to the experimental text (20):

(20)   Machines imitate. One example of this is of a soaring bird next to an airplane. Walking is the one thing that had resisted imitation. ~~Ead~~ People argued whether a horse left the ground with its whole body when he ran. Eadward Baybridge (?) said that the horse didn't. This holds true for humans, cheetah, etc. There are two major differences between static and dynamic balance. The first deals with the definition of stability [...] The second difference deals w/ momentum and speed. One example of this is when a fast moving car suddenly stops and lurches forward. Everything would work out if we just relaxed.

[space of about 1 inch]

The definition of stability also talks about having a sufficient base. [end] [125C]

The learner struggled through the initial portion of the recall, although later she gained some control and was able to relate the gist of the discussion of balance in a rather cohesive albeit somewhat general manner. At some point, though, she stopped writing about the experimental text and left us with the mysterious and unprecedented remark underlined above. It is difficult to say, then, how she defined her goal at that point, unless was it just to "write anything." What is interesting, however, is that the apparent shift in orientation resulted in her ultimately being able to continue her discussion on the subject of balance, as is indicated by the following and last line of the protocol.

Finally, one learner apparently finished the protocol with a series of dash-like marks that continued from the end of the written recall to the bottom of the page (21):

(21)   En la Villa Salvador many people - - - -

        [plus two additional lines made up of dashes] [205B]

The various shifts in orientation presented in (18-21), illustrate the different ways in which learners were able to continue writing with a reasonable amount of control by virtue of having changed the goal of their activity (and hence the activity itself) to one they were able to achieve. In some cases, such as where a learner provided extra-textual yet pertinent information (18), the new goal seemed to be somewhat related to the general prescribed task of recalling the text. However, other revised actions, such as those seen in (19-21), seem less germane. This brings up the possibility that more than a few learners were most strongly oriented to the task of writing something, whatever that might have been, in order to fill the page.

Momentary Shifts in Orientation: Subgoals

There were some shifts in orientation visible in the protocols that did not seem to suggest that the learners had redefined the goal. Rather, these shifts appear to represent temporary, cognitively-oriented departures from the dominant, socially oriented activity. In these situations, the writers formed a momentary sub-goal that they then attempted to accomplish, during the pursuit of the principal goal. An example of such a sub-goal was the lexical search, which was argued to represent the externalization of a learner's running through the days of the week in order to determine the meaning of *viernes*. Because the experiment was not videotaped, there is no way to know for sure at what exact point the learner realized the lexical search. However, there is evidence to indicate that this subgoal was formed and attempted sometime after the recall had been initiated. There are signs of editing in the body of the protocol (writing that had been scratched out) right before the word "Friday" appears. This seems to show that the learner first generated a lexical item, which she found to be unsatisfactory, and consequently launched a lexical search, thus momentarily orienting herself to a private use of language.

As has been discussed in some detail, several learners left blank spaces in lieu of missing lexical information (22):

(22)   ...democrat ~~Bob~~ ^**Robert** Torricelli (rep from   ) + Bob _____, senator
        from Florida. [204A]

Here, the learner was also faced with a lexical gap, although the problem seemed
to be a memory and not a language problem. In all likelihood, the gap forced the
learner to undertake a lexical search as well. However, unlike the learner mentioned above, he was unsuccessful in his search. Thus, the learner ended this activity and, being unable to offer the missing word(s), simply left blank spaces.

In one instance of a cognitively-oriented sidetrack, the writer momentarily
diverted her attention from relating the text to figuring out a specific problem,
namely the chronology of some of the events mentioned in English newspaper
text (23):

(23)   The newsarticle [sic] ~~entitled~~ about the quasi-dictator Fujimori in Peru reported
        that results of a poll taken of voters leaving polling places pointed towards his
        ~~vict~~ drafting a new constitution by 80 members of parliament. ~~The~~ <u>Fujimori
        seized power April 5, the survey was taking place Nov.22</u>. With Fujimori's vic-
        tory, he would gain international recognition [...]

        There was little violence during the election, despite guerrilla threats, only 2 peo-
        ple were injured when dinamite [sic] was thrown at polling places. In addition,
        many Peruvians turned out to vote even though several large groups expressed
        opposition to the endeavor [end]. [109B]

In the above example (23), the learner interrupted her relating of the newspaper
text to put the elections in some sort of historical context.[4] However, the information, underlined above, while correct, does not seem to follow from the
information which precedes it. Because this protocol shows a relatively high
degree of cohesion overall (unlike, say, (16)), it seems likely that this non-
sequitur simply represents a temporary departure from an otherwise cohesive
and reader-directed recall.

Editing also seems to fit the description of a momentary shift in orientation
and the creation of a subgoal. Numerous examples of editing were presented in
the previous chapters, corresponding to both on-line comprehension as well as to
later changes to the text. In the case of on-line comprehension, learners appear to
temporarily redirect their attention to an immediately preceding segment, as
shown in (24):

(24)   People in one ~~small~~ large shanty town [...] [101B]

In this example, the on-line editing reveals that writing "small" caused the learner
to realize that she was wrong. Furthermore, it shows that her mental activity
momentarily redirected itself at modifying the recall so that it matched what she
had just understood, suggesting a brief shift to a cognitive orientation.

The protocols also revealed several cases in which learners had edited the protocols in order to correct ambiguous pronouns, such as in (25):

(25)   This ^**problem** was solved with the development of slow-motion photography [...] [204]

As argued earlier, the editing in this protocol apparently took place sometime after this sentence was written (perhaps during re-reading) and shows a temporary shift toward the more social orientation of making the recall protocol more acceptable to the reader, by eliminating potential ambiguity.

ORIENTATION TO THE PAGE

In much of the discussion thus far, the private writing features and sometimes the content of the protocols have been used in order to determine properties of the learners' orientation and activity while producing the recall protocols. Now we consider another feature of the protocols: the distribution of writing across the page. It will be shown that the way in which learners utilize both the margin and the text-space (the middle of the page) can inform us further as to the learner's orientation and activity in the task of recall.

The Margin

Various examples of learners' writing in the margin have been presented earlier. The margin was used by several learners at the outset of the writing in order to plan the recall (104C), to copy down, and hence save information (104A, 104B), and in order to execute lexical searches (109A) after the recall had begun. In other words, the margin was seen to be a locus of self-oriented writing. These examples are especially revealing because they suggest that the learners were, at certain points, aware of the private nature of their writing, and chose to realize it outside of the social-looking text they were trying to produce. Thus, at some level the learners were determined to produce a text for someone else, in spite of the necessary cognitive detours.

There was one instance in which a learner used the margin in order to add information to the body of the recall text, which was presumably generated sometime after the point at which it was to be inserted (116A). This learner put the additional information ("before the election") in the margin and then drew arrows to indicate that it belonged inside the text. In this way, the learner indicated that she understood that the reader-directed text was contained within the boundaries of the textspace.

Most of the private writing activity, however, went on within the confines of the text space, rather than in the margin. This may suggest a lack of awareness on the part of most learners as to the private nature of their writing. However, it may also be due in large part to the fact that for many the entire writing of the protocol was a cognitive exercise. The learners were under such pressure that they probably had little cognitive distance with which to form subgoals and even less to separate them from what was an essentially private text.[5]

The Textspace

The textspace, or the main area in the middle of the page where the body of the recalls were written, was often, but not always characterized by division into paragraphs. The division, when present, was marked either with indentation or with a space between paragraphs, the latter being the case of the three experimental texts. One learner, (203) whose recall of the expository text was previously characterized as a complaint, further marked his paragraphs with dashes and references to the paragraphs in the original text. This is consistent with his postulated orientation to point out the stylistic weakness of specific sections of the text.

It may be that in other cases, division of the recall into separate paragraphs is a reflection of the learners' orientation toward the reproduction of the original texts. However it seems likely that the relative difficulty of the three texts was also a factor. It is interesting to note that such division was more likely to occur with the English texts than with the Spanish text. Thus, the purposeful division of the recall into paragraphs required at least a degree of comprehension and control that was beyond the learners after reading the Spanish text. That is, learners needed to have understood enough information to warrant separate paragraphs and, furthermore, to be sufficiently in control as to organize what they had understood into cohesive chunks.

It is also further interesting to note that, at least for the recalls of the Spanish text, the undelineated protocols were also those that exhibited multiple manifestations of private writing, specifically, marked with problematic uses of tense, aspect and focus. Thus, if learners were involved in the activity of trying to figure out the text through writing about it, they were less likely and perhaps unable to orient themselves to producing distinct and cohesive paragraphs. To put it another way, the learners were involved in a different activity, namely trying to comprehend the original text, which did not always leave time for producing a cohesive and structured recall text.

A frequent characteristic of the protocols of the English newspaper text was the presence of a separate paragraph at the end of the recall text. This paragraph often consisted of only one sentence having to do specifically with the fact that the results of the elections discussed in the text were expected the following day. What is particularly intriguing is that this was sometimes the case for otherwise undelineated recalls and, furthermore, this paragraph or sentence was often located at a considerable physical distance (anywhere from one to four inches) from the body of the recall text. While this particular feature of the recalls seems surprising, it may in fact have been caused by the set-up of the original text itself.

The English newspaper text was made up of eight distinct paragraphs which, as stated earlier, were separated by a space of blank text. The last paragraph of the text consisted of a single sentence and made reference to the anticipated results of the election: "Official results are expected Monday." It seems likely then that both its brevity and recency combined to make that particular phrase and its preceding space especially salient in the minds of the learners, who were perhaps then better able to remember both the content of the phrase and the fact that it was somehow separate from the preceding text. This appears to have been the case for even those learners who were so busy deciphering the text during the recall that they were unable to delineate any other paragraph in the protocol.

In the recalls of the expository text, there are additional and varied examples of blank spaces at the end of the main recall text followed by further writing. However, these spaces seem to reflect the learner's awareness of a shift in focus. Consider the following excerpt (26):

(26)   Static & dynamic motion have two differences; first static
        [Space of about two inches]

        Machines must have both static & dynamic motion in order to walk. [end]
        [109C]

Interestingly, the second to last line of the protocol is left unfinished, suggesting that the learner was unable to complete that particular thought. Specifically, she could not explain the first, much less generate the second, difference between static and dynamic motion. However, she did leave a space for the missing information and went on to recover more details from the text. The example, then, is reminiscent of those learners who left spaces (underlined and otherwise) for missing lexical items in the text of the recall protocols (i.e. the names of the legislators in the Spanish text, or the village mentioned in the English newspaper text). Thus, while the gap is somewhat of a higher level, (e.g. the discourse versus the lexicon), the learner in (26) dealt with the problem in a similar way. Unable to generate the missing information, she left a space for it, and reoriented herself to the activity of recalling more of the text. The blank space may be the learner's way of signaling that she realized that there was information missing and, furthermore, that the subsequent information did not follow logically from what immediately preceded it. In a sense, it is a graphic representation of her "jumping ahead."

The remaining examples do not include an unfinished sentence like the one in (26), but do seem to involve the same sort of shift in focus in the recall (27-28), or in the case of (29), a return to focus:

(27)   [...] With humans and animals which remove one more legs from the stability of the ground consistantly [sic], th they must be able to correct for momentary imbalances.

[space of about one inch]
Velocity also must be considered. With constant [...] [end] [116C]

(28)   Dynamic balance has intermittent times of tipping when the subject is off-balance but, overtime, this effect is neutralized.

[space of about three inches]
In the study of running, one mustn't limit the definition of balance. [end] [124C]

(29)   One example of this is when a fast moving car suddenly stops and lurches forward. Everything would work it we just relaxed.

[space of about one inch]
The definition of stability also talks about having a sufficient base. [125C]

In these examples, the last line of the text came after a space of one to three inches following the main body of the recall text. What is particularly interesting is that the learners did not otherwise divide the main text into paragraphs, which seems to support the idea that their intention was to somehow distance the final comments from the text. One reason for that might be that the learners realized that their concluding statements did not follow logically from the preceding information. That seems particularly obvious in the case of (29), where the penultimate sentence of the protocols, as was argued earlier, clearly represents a temporary departure from the task of recalling or even of trying to understand the experimental text. Thus, the learners marked that disjuncture graphically.

Again, it is difficult to say with absolute certainty when and how these blank spaces came about. Drawing on the content of the surrounding text, however, it is not unreasonable to suggest that they represent a sort of pause in the learners recall activity. That is, the learners externalized all that they were able to and stopped. At some point afterwards, they were able to generate further information, but realizing that it would not be cohesive to simply add it to the main body of the text, they marked the temporal and contextual distance with an empty space. This explanation finds support in the following protocol, where the learner marked shifts at the end of the protocols, not with spaces but with new paragraphs (30):

(30)   [...] Rebels through [sic] sticks of dynamite and bombs at the polls and two people sustained injuries, but there were no deaths. In one of the shabbiest towns, [...] voters walked through the sandy streets to vote in a run down school house.

Results are expected Monday
He'll attribute his win to his actions April 5. [113B]

With the exception of the last two lines/paragraphs, this protocol was otherwise undelineated, as the learner had not divided the main divided the main body of the text in separate paragraphs. It has already been suggested that the saliency of the information regarding the election results may explain its distance from the body of the text. However, the question is, how can the last line of the protocol, also symbolically distanced as a new paragraph, be explained? Again, the line seems to represent information that was generated by the learner after she had written what she probably thought was the last line of her recall. She must have realized that this new information did not belong at the end of the text. In fact, it probably belonged somewhere in the middle. Her choice was to either suppress the information, or some how mark it as different. Perhaps based on her impression that she ought to write all that she could, she choose the latter option.

The examples in (26-30), then, represent additional and, in a sense, belated, comprehension on the part of the learners. However, those who were able to maintain a more social-orientation during their writing activity were likewise able to orient themselves toward this new information in such a way that it reveals their intention to write down everything they could think of as part of a social and thus logically ordered text.

The recall protocols of the English expository text contained several instances of this marked "later" comprehension. In contrast, there was one example each in the newspaper recalls. One possible explanation is that while the English expository text may have been easy in the sense that the language was understandable at least at the lexical and syntactic level, the content was sufficiently difficult that many needed to work it out in writing. Thus, it was very often the case with this text that the learners were comprehending major portions of the text while they were thinking about it, both during and after writing. The English newspaper text, on the other hand, was more transparent in that the learners were able to understand not only most words but also most of the sentences in the text. Thus, many were able to actually comprehend the text as a text during the reading. For this text, then, writing was less likely to be oriented toward the need to comprehend. The reading of the Spanish newspaper text was probably like the reading of the English expository text in that difficulty was first encountered at the time of reading. However, the language of the text was opaque for many learners, and while the writing of the protocols did reveal on-going comprehension at a different level, the writers were not able to count on a lot of given information. Thus, when the writing stopped, for many, so did comprehension.

This explanation seems to hold, especially in the case of the reading and recall of the Spanish text, given that the only instance of later comprehension in these protocols consists of single propositions, rather than complete sentences, as was the case in (26-30). Recall, for example, the learner, considered earlier, who ended her protocol with a short list of propositions (31):

(31)   600 citizens?
       Torricelli—N.J. Senator? [125A]

Ultimately, the learner was only able to conjure up individual propositions, lacking the necessary information to put them into context. However, she apparently had enough control at this point, perhaps because she become involved in a less demanding activity, order to signal said shift. This is significant because not all learners, despite shifting orientation, were able to mark the changes. Recall, for example, the learner whose engagement in the task of comprehending the experimental task led her to produce an outline. That she did not have the presence of mind to signal this change is consistent with the extreme private orientation she maintained for the duration of the recall.

Instances of more dramatic shifts in orientation can be seen in the following examples (32-33):

(32)   I think this was the last sentence.

       [space of about 4 inches]
       A cruel thing to make students read. [203C]

(33)   Static vs. dynamic balance, when in static balance a tripod-like three limbs in contact with the ground is necessary. Center of gravity has to be over the legs and tipping at all can't be present - - -

       Out of time [205C]

The space in the excerpt in (32) is clearly consist with the shift in orientation indicated by the content of this learner's concluding remarks. As was discussed earlier, the learner was oriented toward recalling some of the content of the text as well as criticizing its stylistic faults. He was particularly concerned with representing each section of the text graphically. The final comment, separated from the body of the recall text by a space, represents a change in orientation in that he switched from talking about a section of the text to talking about the entire text. Furthermore, and more importantly, he was no longer involved in the recall of any content of the text or with representing any section of the text. Thus, the intention to critique—or perhaps even to complain—as realized in the last sentence of the text, was no longer embedded in the task of recalling or reproducing the text. Rather, it had become a unique and separate goal, as its positioning significantly below the recall text would seem to suggest.

In the same way, the final comment in (33) does not seem to be a direct manifestation of the activity of recalling the experimental text. Rather it is a remark perhaps, like the final declaration in (32), directed at the experimenter, with which the learner explains his status in the activity. It seems reasonable to imagine that the learner was busy writing when the experimenter called time. The learner, left without the opportunity to write down any further information that he might still have, shifted his orientation toward explaining that he was cut off. Thus, he informs the reader why the recall texts ends where it does.[6] By leaving a blank space (and also by using larger script) the learner clearly indicates that this information is not to be understood as part of the recall text itself.

ORIENTATION AND THE LEXICON

This section briefly discusses what some of the lexical items in the recall protocols can reveal about the activity in which the learners were engaged as well as their orientation to that activity. In all three sets of protocols, we can see that the difficulties experienced at the time of writing caused the learners to orient themselves away from the language of the recalls. As a result, the protocols exhibit distortions in the learners' language that one would ordinarily not expect from native speakers. Some properties of the Spanish recalls illustrate quite clearly the language problems that the learners encountered while reading a text in their L2. Properties of the English expository recalls give evidence that the learners were led astray by even the seemingly common-place vocabulary of that text.

The Spanish Newspaper Text

A quick glance at the content of the recall protocols from the Spanish newspaper text reveals that most learners faced great difficulty at both the syntactic and lexical level while reading the text. Many learners had little access to the syntactic (i.e., sentence level) information. Thus, instead of being able to parse actual sentences, many learners instead formed sentence-level propositions by drawing on various lexical items, in addition to world knowledge. Unfortunately, however, the learners often misinterpreted key lexical items, and thus rendered recall protocols that differed greatly from the original text. For example, *terceros países*, "other" or literally "third countries" was most often understood as "third world countries." Likewise, *empresas subsidiarias*, literally, "subsidiaries," was frequently read as "subsidies." For many, then, the text incorrectly came to involve "U.S. subsidies to third world countries," an interpretation in which world knowledge likely played a role.

Often when learners correctly interpreted different lexical items, they did so with a certain degree of doubt, as can be seen in the following examples (34-36):

(34)   "Castro should/must fall." [126C]
(35)   He did this [...] to gain (keep) the support of Cuban-americans in Florida. [120A]
(36)   Bush initially opposed the law, anticipating its refusal or opposition by other countries. [203A]

In each of these three examples, the learners provided two options for a particular item, which shows that they were probably not entirely certain of either one of the choices. Interestingly, the indecision in (34), may have derived from the perceived ambiguity of the word *deber* in the original text, which can mean either "should" or "must."

The protocols of the Spanish text, and to a lesser extent those of the other two experimental texts, were characterized by what will be referred to here as peculiar language. By this we mean language, mostly words or phrases, which, given that the learners were writing in their native language, seemed a bit out of place or oddly phrased. Some of these peculiarities reflect the Spanish of the original text, while others seem to have resulted from the overall difficulty in completing the recall. Consider for example the following excerpts (37-40):

(37)   He wants that all of Cuba will be united <u>under liberty</u>. [125A]
(38)   [...] until all Cubans are able to live, united, <u>under freedom</u>. [111A]
(39)   [...] France, Mexico, Canada and the <u>Reino Unido</u>. [204A]
(40)   President Busch Bush, this past <u>Octobre</u>, endorsed a bill [...] [124A]

In (37) and (38), the use of the preposition "under" with "liberty" and "free-dom" reflects a literal translation of the proposition in the Spanish rendering *bajo libertad* "under liberty," in spite of the fact that in English the concept would more likely be rendered using the preposition "in," as in "in freedom." This shows, then, that some learners were unable to distance themselves enough from the language of the original text to produce felicitous English phrases. In (39) and (40), the learners were unable to distance themselves at all from the language of the text, and instead could only write down the Spanish words.

Other peculiar words and phrases did not seem to derive directly from the language of the original text. Consider for example, the following excerpts (41-42):

(41)   [...] he said that <u>US aid to Cuba would not occur</u> [...] [117A]
(42)   [...] support from <u>Cuban Florida residents</u> . [202B]

The above underlined phrases, while understandable, both seem odd. They do not correspond literally to anything in the original text, suggesting that the locus of the immediate problem is not the language of the news article. Rather, recalling the experimental text was simply so difficult that it caused a distortion of the learners' own language. It is likely that at times the learners were so strongly ori-ented toward trying to understand the propositional content of the Spanish text, that they were forced to pay less attention to some aspects of their writing, such as the exact choice of lexical items. The writers lacked the cognitive distance that would have been necessary to ensure that the language of the recall text was appropriate.

The English Newspaper Text

The language of the recall protocols of the English newspaper text indicates that the learners experienced considerably less difficulty with the lexicon of that text, which is essentially what one would expect from the reading of a non-technical, first language text. As was discussed in Chapter 4, the learners were notably more confident about specific lexical items and cases of doubt were limited to two proper names (the village and Maoist group mentioned).

The recalls were not without signs of peculiarity. However, only one set of examples seems traceable to the language of the original text. The remaining examples may again derive from the overall difficulty experienced by the writers during the recall of the text. Consider first the following examples of text-induced anomalies (43-45):

(43)   In one of the shabbiest towns [...] [113B]
(44)   In one of the smallest ^**shabbiest** towns [...] [104B]
(45)   [...] who will redesign the Peruvian Constitution. [124B]

Curiously, there were several references to a "shabby town" throughout the protocols, examples of which are given in (43) and (44). The original text itself spoke of a large "shanty town." The fact that in the protocols a learner referred to either a "shabby town" or a "shanty town" but not to a "shabby shanty town" suggests that some learners simply understood or even read "shabby" at the time of reading and later recalled it. That no learner expressed doubt over the denomination "shabby" in the recall protocols is evidence that such a description was coherent with their view of the world. The choice of "redesign" (45) is somewhat anomalous because constitutions are not usually "designed" but it may have been triggered by the use of "rewrite" in the original text.[7]

As in the recall protocols of the Spanish newspaper text, the recalls of the English newspaper article contained several oddly constructed phrases or peculiar lexical choices as shown in the following examples (46-49):

(46)   [...] a set of Congress people [...] [102B]
(47)   It was worried whether or not voting would be safe. [102B]
(48)   2 were hurt but there were no casualties. [108B]
(49)   small ~~MShin~~ incidents of bombs were committed [...] [124B]

Again, these phrases have no antecedents in the experimental texts and thus seem to be a product of the difficulty of the task. It is likely that, for most learners, reading and recalling the English newspaper text was significantly easier at a local level than reading and recalling the Spanish newspaper text. Furthermore, fewer learners were engaged in trying to understand the English text than the Spanish text at the time of writing. Nonetheless, reading and recalling the English newspaper text was by no means an easy task and learners were apparently not always able to pay close attention to their choice of vocabulary. Some learners, therefore, were more strongly oriented to higher level goals, namely recalling the content in a coherent manner, or even to comprehending the text, than they were toward the lower or lexical level of their own writing. Simply put, the learners were too engrossed in attending to other more immediate, problems to always worry about the language of the recalls.

The English Expository Text

As with the protocols of the newspaper texts, the protocols of the expository text exhibited language that can best be characterized as peculiar, as illustrated by the following examples (50-52):

(50)   For example, a soaring bird metaphors an airplane. [113C]
(51)   Lately, scientists have pondered the plausibility of a machine that can walk. [102C]
(52)   To study how animals and humans ambulate [...] [124C]

Again, these oddly constructed phrases and peculiar lexical choices may be understood as a consequence of the overall difficulty of producing a recall for that particular experimental text.

   One of the most interesting features of these protocols, nevertheless, was the evidence that some learners did have significant trouble with certain lexical items used in the technical discussion of the text. However, the problem was not that there was a lot of scientific vocabulary used in the discussion. Rather, it was the technical use of some relatively familiar words which appeared to perplex the learners. That would seem to account for some of the hesitancy and lack of certainty expressed by learners via the use of quotation marks or interrogative signs regarding what appear to be commonplace words, as can be seen in the following examples (53-58):

(53)   In static balancing, an object must have 3 bases of support; a "tripod". [123C]
(54)   They have a tripod effect with feet firmly planted at all times. [101C]
(55)   "Ballistic motion" is difficult for a machine to imitate. [121C]
(56)   This also deals with the 'tipping' idea. [125C]
(57)   [...] the legs act as a tripod as the vehicle is 'crawling' along. [118C]
(58)   Statistical stability (?) is when all legs, or whatever, are touching the ground. [127C]

The word "tripod" was used in the text in its most general sense, that is, to refer to something having three bases or limbs of support. However, the quotation marks in (53) seem to indicate that the learners were somewhat uneasy about using the term in that context, suggesting that they had interpreted the term more restrictedly, that is, as referring specifically, to the more familiar three-legged device used to support photographic equipment.[8] The phrasing "tripod effect" in (54) supports this analysis, as it seems to imply that the learner understood that somehow "tripod" was being used as an analogy—outside of its normal context—for the three-legged base of support discussed in the text.

The quotation marks in (55-57) also seem to suggest that, for some reason, the learners were uncertain about the use of certain words in the content presented in the expository text. The word "statistical" and the question mark following it in (58) are particularly interesting for several reasons. First, this excerpt is one of several instances in which learners read "statistical" for "static," ostensibly much in the same way that some learners mistook "shabby town" for "shanty town." Interestingly, however, it is one of the few instances in which a learner expressed some uncertainty about recalling this item. Although it was incorrect, the term "statistical" must have fit better into the learners' perception of what this scientific texts should be about than did other words like "tipping" and "tripod."

Parallel to the way in which "tripod" was understood in a restricted sense by some learners, the term "vehicle," used in the text to refer to any device capable of motion, was rather narrowly interpreted by some to mean "car." In addition to engendering uncertainty, the everyday or naive interpretation of these two words in particular sometimes caused learners to attribute seemingly strange statements to the text, as following examples illustrate (59-60).

(59)   For a car to remain balanced during stability it must be "on a tripod". For dynamic it can be on 2 wheels [...] [119C]
(60)   A car must have 3 of its 4 tires on the ground to maintain stability, and so the human must have his/her feet tipped to maintain stability. [107C]

Both learners have interpreted "vehicle" to refer specifically to "car" (which in fact was not mentioned in the text) and have further analyzed tripod in terms of that interpretation, namely as referring to three of the car's wheels. This reading, however, leads both writers to generate statements that are at odds with what they must know about cars. Namely, that they are not likely to have only three wheels on the ground and be in motion at the same time. Thus, the learners' restricted interpretations have caused them to produce distorted statements about the real world, which, instead of forcing a re-analysis of the relevant lexical items, allows them to maintain their original analysis.

The examples in (59) and (60), as well as those in (53-58) are particularly interesting because they reveal that these learners approached the text not as experts. Instead, they approached the text as people with only everyday knowledge of the items in the text. This is somewhat surprising, considering that the learners were all college students who more than likely had more than some exposure to and, thus perhaps had some familiarity with, reading (and writing about) scientific texts. Nonetheless, it may have been the case that the time constraint of the experiment helped to orient them toward a more familiar way of knowing. This would be somewhat akin to the learner in Appel and Lantolf (1994) who referred to the scientific text used in that experiment as a story. Thus, in difficult situations, people return to ontogenetically earlier ways of knowing and approaching the world.

SUMMARY

In this chapter, we have looked at the learners' different and changing orientations to the task of producing a written recall protocol. Overall, the data reveal that learners exhibited distinct orientations to the task based on their assessment of the task and the difficulties they encountered as they initiated and worked through the task. Increase (or decrease) in difficulty was shown to be one factor which altered the learners' assessment of the task and thus forced a change in activity

Importantly, it was found that orientation is not categorical but rather multi-faceted and fluid. Thus, learners often revealed both private and social features in their writing as they struggled to maintain control in what was supposed to be a social task. Also, the private speech feature of the learners' writing indicated that orientation continued to shift throughout the protocols as learners reacted to difficulty and gaps in information. In most cases, writers shifted to comprehending through writing, rather than recalling. Sometimes, learners responded to the cognitive difficulty encountered by altering their activity more drastically, opting to pursue a more feasible goal.

In an interesting departure from the analysis of purely linguistic (i.e. grammatical) features, it was shown that the actual physical location of writing on the page could provide information about the learners' orientation and activity. Specifically, it was found that, in some cases, writers purposefully used the margins of the page in order to externalize certain meaning-constructing and even planning activity. Furthermore, sometimes learners even manipulated the textspace to show cognitive distance between writing caused by changes in orientation.

Finally, an analysis of some of the lexical features of the protocols showed that some learners were not able to orient themselves to the individual words they were producing, presumably because they were too busy attending to other more immediate aspects of the activity. As a result, the writers' own language was often distorted, a reflection of the overall difficulty of the task. Also, a look at the way in which learners interpreted vocabulary items from the expository text indicated that some learners were not able to orient themselves to the task as experts reading a scientific text. Rather, the difficulty of the task forced them to approach the task from an everyday or lay person perspective, again proving that in difficult situations, people resort to more familiar and ontogenetically more primitive ways of being and knowing, of which private speech is only one example.

NOTES

[1]   There were actually two learners who interpreted the written task directions in this way, although learner 106 was the only one who then oriented himself to translation and memorization. It is important to point out that a quantitative study would in all likelihood have excluded these learners from the analysis, because their performance would be considered too different from that of the group. The present study, however, takes as its premise that the activity of each learner is, at some level, unique, and is precisely concerned with discovering this singularity.

[2]   An alternative explanation might be that the learner was in fact oriented toward memorization but was unsuccessful. This, however, is not consistent with the assumption that the English newspaper text was relatively easier than either of the two other experimental texts.

[3]   It also possible that this orientation arose in part from the learner's individual learning style, which is in fact hinted at by this learner's on-task behavior in the classroom. In particular the learner was heavily reliant on his dictionary and could often be found translating even task instructions.

[4]   The original newspaper article mentioned both events, but not did mention or compare them together, as this learner has done. Rather, elections, the focus of the article, were mentioned at the beginning and Fujimori's takeover, in this context background material, was related later.

[5]   See DiCamilla and Lantolf (1994) for a discussion of the problems that novice writers have separating planning to write from actual writing.

[6]   What is not known, of course, is why the learner wished to communicate that information to the researcher. It may have been a face-saving strategy

[7]   Except, of course, for the figurative sense: The constitution was designed to protect civil liberties.

[8]   It seems unlikely that, alternatively, the learners were expressing doubt as to the spelling of the word, as might have been the case with the proper names mentioned in the experimental texts (i.e. Torricelli, Muybridge etc.).

Conclusion

By way of conclusion, three particularly relevant issues will be discussed. The first deals with the question of linguistic mediation and control in light of the evidence of private writing found in the recall protocols. The second issue is concerned with the proposed distinction between task and activity. After considerable discussion regarding the shifts in orientation and activity evident in the protocols, it is appropriate—perhaps surprisingly so—to entertain, at least briefly the possibility that the learners, in fact, did not change their activity at all. Finally, the third point to be discussed deals with the implications of this study for reading research and for general pedagogy, as the analysis of the recall protocols employed in this study has had as one of its principal goals a deeper understanding of what it means to read and recall a text, an understanding which ought to benefit researchers and practitioners alike.

PRIVATE WRITING AND SEMIOTIC MEDIATION

The analysis of the linguistic and discursive features of the recall protocols revealed abundant examples of private writing. The particular private writing features were found in various amounts and to differing degrees across the three sets of protocols. This finding has been attributed, in large part, to the language and content variables which distinguished the three experimental texts and apparently rendered the reading of each text different. Consistent with previous studies in this framework, the private writing features were interpreted as indicative of the difficulties encountered by the learners in their attempt to produce a recall protocol.

Moreover, the language of the protocols provided evidence of the strategic and problem-solving nature of speech activity or, in the case at hand, of the learners' writing activity, as the learners were obliged to mediate their thinking with external semiotic tools in order to complete the task. The learners were thus shown to express and cope with difficulty in the task through the strategic use of their most powerful cognitive tool: linguistic mediation.

Many of the private writing features observed previously in the literature, such as particular uses of tense and aspect, epistemic modality, ambiguous reference, and focus, were present in the recall protocols. It was shown, however, that the way in which these particular features manifest themselves depends to a great extent on the task being undertaken and the relative degree of control the writer possesses. Thus, the study ought not to be seen as contributing to a definitive taxonomy of private writing forms. Rather, it should be viewed as indicating how language can be used to enable thinking, problem solving and the like, according to the cognitive demands and orientation of the speaker or writer, that is, as semiotic mediation.

In addition to the well described characteristics of private speech, several other private uses of language were discovered in the recall protocols. For example, vague language was found to be used strategically by the learners as a way of structuring a discourse based on little and uncertain information. Additionally, it was found that even the location of the writing on the page could be indicative of the learners' orientation and activity. Furthermore, it appeared that sometimes that space was purposefully manipulated by the learners in an attempt to carry out their activity.

Crucially, the analysis of the private writing features revealed that the learners were simultaneously engaged in both privately and socially oriented writing activity. In other words, the language of protocols reflected an interweaving of social and private writing, although sometimes this balance was seen to favor one function or the other. This suggests that at some point the categorical distinction between cognitive and communicative linguistic activity may need to be reconsidered. Frawley (1992) has already observed that private speech may appear as a communicative act. Vygotsky (1986) claimed that mental activity is the way in which we organize all our physical and psychological behavior and, furthermore, that this activity is semiotically mediated. In this view, speech activity must be about constructing our mental, social, and physical space—a state of affairs which seems to imply that mind is always to some degree external. Thus, the question is whether there is any linguistic activity that does not have an organizing or self-regulatory function. It may be the case that all external language activity, in spite of the lack of aberrant linguistic forms, is private or regulatory to some degree. Thus, what is currently considered signs of private speech may only be evidence of extreme cases of cognitive distress. In the same way, the criteria of aberrance or oddness, which is ultimately predicated on the prescriptive norms of written language, may also need to be reevaluated.

ACTIVITY AND THE SOCIOCULTURAL SETTING

The analysis of the private writing forms in the recall protocols revealed that the orientation of the learners was not homogenous at the outset nor stable throughout the task. Rather, the learners' writing activity appeared to be oriented toward different goals at different points in the recall. The learners' orientation was seen to undergo shifts, based on their assessment of the task and the difficulties they encountered as they initiated and worked through the task. The differences in orientation at the start of writing, the on-line shifts in orientation and apparent modifications to the goal of the activity (e.g. from recalling to understanding) were interpreted as further evidence for Coughlin and Duff's (1994) proposal that task-generated activity is not predictable, controllable, or homogenous across learners or time. Moreover, it was determined (based primarily on the postulation that some learners had altered their goals) that they had been engaged in one and the same task, but in different activities. Crucially, then, the learners in this study were found to have behaved as true participants, that is, as agents, actively engaged in shaping their own activity.

That analysis notwithstanding, it is nonetheless possible to examine the learners' activity from a different perspective and observe that there was little change in activity. When one takes into consideration the larger discursive space in which the learners' activity took place, namely, an academic setting, it becomes apparent that the actual goal of the learners may have been very different from what the researcher had intended and, furthermore, that goal was relatively constant across the learners and throughout the tasks.

No learner refused to participate nor abandoned the experiment midstream (although one, as will be recalled, did complain about an experimental text in his recall). Furthermore, no learner failed to produce at least some sort of written text. Yet, the abundance of private writing phenomena and the propositional content of the recall protocols suggests that for all but a few learners, completing the recall task involved a good deal of difficulty. That was true, of course, to a greater degree in the case of the Spanish newspaper text and the English expository text, but even the recall of the English newspaper text cannot be said to have been easy. Furthermore, it was evident that some learners were simply not very successful in recalling more than a few propositions. Taking into consideration the apparent difficulty of producing a recall protocol and the fact that the learners were in no way obliged to participate in or complete the experimental procedures, the question that needs to be answered is why the learners continued to write.

One fairly plausible explanation for the learners' persistence in the task, even when they had reached the point where what they were producing was incoherent or seemingly irrelevant to the task as set by the researcher, is that the primary goal of all learners was not to recall the text nor even to understand it through writing. Rather, their goal might have been that of simply complying with what they believed to be the researcher's wishes: Produce a written text. In short, the learners were in all likelihood most strongly oriented to the goal of filling up the page for the researcher, in whatever way possible. The goal was indeed a demanding one, but was not abandoned even in the face of difficulty. The fact that the learners in some cases changed their actions some (e.g. in going from writing about the text to writing about the outside world) is irrelevant in the sense that it did not substantially alter the learners' activity: As long as the macro-level goal remained constant, the learners' activity can be interpreted as having been stable and homogenous. Thus, the learners were engaged in the same task and seemingly the same—or at least very similar—activity.[1]

The preceding analysis of the learners' macro-level activity is consistent with the sociocultural context in which the experiment was administered. Namely, the experiment was conducted by an instructor (in most cases the learners' own instructor), in a classroom, during class time and, perhaps most importantly, in the context of a pervasive educational setting—the university in which the learners were enrolled as part of their participation in another activity, formal schooling. Therefore, in spite of the orientation tentatively suggested by the researcher, it was the learners' own sociocultural setting that may have been most instrumental in forming the goal which defined their activity. Importantly, it should be pointed out that this analysis does not, however, refute the "same task, different activity" characterization of the learners" behavior maintained earlier. Rather, it is an account of their activity from a different level, and an indication of the multi-layered nature of human mental activity. Thus, it may be the case that the learners formed different subgoals (i.e. memorization, recalling) as part of their overall activity directed at accomplishing their macro-level orientation.

IMPLICATIONS FOR RESEARCH AND PEDAGOGY

Finally, the concerns of reading research and practice are addressed. All three sets of recall protocols provided evidence of the learners' on-going comprehension of the experimental text in the act of writing. Along with Appel and Lantolf's (1994) findings, as well as recent work by Kintsch (1993) and Markovà (1992), these results are consistent with the claim that language use is a meaning-making, as opposed to meaning-relating, endeavor. What is particularly interesting is that evidence of on-going comprehension was found in protocols whose language reflected the learners' struggle to comprehend the text, as well as in those protocols which offered little signs of private writing and instead suggested that the learners were very much in control of the information of the text. Thus, semiotically mediated meaning-making does not only occur when learners are attempting to understand the text at the time of writing, but also in those cases where learners had apparently been able to construct meaning at the time of reading. Meaning-making, then, is simply a consequence (or perhaps the purpose) of writing activity.

The evidence of on-going comprehension, when considered in a meaning-construction framework, suggests that recall protocols simply are not the clean measure of text comprehension that some would like them to be, precisely because they attempt to measure something that no longer exists at the time of writing—the comprehension model elaborated at the time of reading. Most researchers assume that learners will be able to reconstruct this model, unaffected, by creating a written or oral "recall." However, this position is simply not tenable. The protocol data of this study overwhelming show that the recall text in-production is itself another act of meaning-construction, which will interact with the intended "recall" of the prior comprehension model.

This understanding of recall, however, in no way is meant to argue that recall data is uninteresting or invalid. Recall protocols can be a rich source of data regarding the meaning-constructing activity of reading and the meaning-constructing activity of producing a recall text. In fact, it has been shown here that an analysis of private writing features can allow the researcher to discriminate to some extent between meaning constructed at the time of reading and later (re)constructed at the time of writing, and meaning which seems to have its origin in the recall activity.

What may be discouraging news for some reading researchers may actually have positive and useful implications for practitioners. The data in this study have indicated that language activity facilitates on-going comprehension, a finding which is of potential consequence for those who struggle with second language texts. For example, post- reading activities may actually be as important as the pre-reading activities that have enjoyed so much attention in recent pedagogical and experimental literature (Appel & Lantolf, 1994). It would not be fair, however, to say that post-reading exercises are not already being used by teachers. Nonetheless, these activities often have the goal of allowing the teacher to determine by whom and how well the assigned text was read and "understood," rather than to help the students understand what they had read (i.e. construct coherent meaning from texts) or encouraging them to position themselves in relation to the text (Kramsch & Nolden, 1994).

In this particular study, increased comprehension was shown to arise in written language activity, a finding which suggests that classroom reading exercises featuring a writing component may be useful. Bernhardt (1991b) does, in fact, argue for the pedagogical use of recall protocols. However, she advocates using written recall primarily as an assessment tool, by which teachers, through a qualitative analysis, are able to pinpoint the source (e.g. lexicon, syntax) of the students' errors. Without negating the value of Bernhardt's recommendation, it seems reasonable to propose that recall-like tasks are important because of the potential benefit they pose to the readers, who may actually come to construct new meaning through their writing activity.

Although the writing in this study was in the learners' native language and involved a specific task (that of producing a written recall protocol) the data to be found here have implications for both L1 and L2 writing in response to other tasks. If, as has been argued, writing promotes comprehension, then second language learners should be encouraged to engage in writing activities in different tasks and content areas with the purpose of facilitating understanding and learning. That is, learners should be encouraged to engage in process writing, where the goal of the writing activity is to function as a learning device. Examples of process-writing tasks include, but are not limited to, reading logs, focused and unfocused free writing, and interpretive paraphrase, and, like the recall protocol, can be assigned to students in order to facilitate learning about different content areas (Tchudi, 1986).

Process-writing tasks ought to be distinguished from content-writing tasks (i.e. producing a position paper, a report, commentary, etc. see Tchudi, 1986) at least in theory, because the goal of former is the activity or the process itself, whereas the goal of the latter is usually the final, written product. The data in this study have shown that writing under stress leads one to distort one's own native language and to use seemingly odd forms in order to externally mediate and thus facilitate the activity of comprehension. It is reasonable to assume and, in fact, it has been shown in numerous studies of private speech (such as those discussed in Chapter 2), that private writing occurs in the L2 as well.[2] Thus, process-writing tasks in the second language ought to contain examples of aberrant forms that should be interpreted as evidence of the writer's externalized cognitive processes. However, learner performance in process-writing tasks should be evaluated on the success of the process, and not on the grammatical accuracy of the product.

Of course, private writing will invariably be found in content-writing tasks, in spite of the teacher's expectations that the learners produce error-free compositions. Again, this private writing is indicative of the writers' on-going comprehension processes as they endeavor to produce a coherent and cohesive text in the second language. However, knowledge of the mediational properties of language and particularly of writing, as expressed in Sociocultural Theory, should provide the teacher with a framework for interpreting learners' content-writing, and hopefully, for providing instruction in distinguishing between the planning or drafting process from that of final writing.

NOTES

[1]   Vygotsky and Leontiev both argued that all human activity was unique, because the conditions of any activity, in that they involve real people with unique sociocultural histories, are necessarily distinct. However, by looking at what Leontiev refers to as the determining features of an activity, namely, its goal, it is possible to compare activities and judge their relative degree of similarity.

[2]   Indeed, some of the cognitive load of writing to comprehend in the target language may come from the difficulty of using an unfamiliar tool in the task of comprehension.

Appendix A:
List of Symbols

The following notations have been used in the typed transcription of the written recall data collected in this study:

~~strike through~~	text was crossed out but is still legible
~~xxx~~	text was crossed out and rendered illegible
^**bold word**	bolded word(s) inserted inserted above and/or after the immediately preceding, unbolded word
^***bold italic word***	bolded and italicized word(s) inserted above and/or after previously inserted material

Appendix B:
Task Instructions

READING COMPREHENSION TASK

You are participating in a experiment looking at how people read in a foreign language. You will be asked to read three separate texts.

On the following page there is a text in Spanish. You will be given 4 minutes to read the text—you may read it as many times as you wish, but you may not take notes. After the four minutes are up, you will be asked to turn the page over and to write down in ENGLISH everything that you can remember about what you have just read. You will have 6 minutes to write.

We ask that you write in pen. If you wish to change something that you have written, please just put a single line though it, but please do not obliterate it completely.

Appendix C:
Texts Used in the Study

EE UU endurece el embargo contra Cuba con la "ley Torricelli"

Miami, EEUU. 28 octubre. El presidente de Estados Unidos, George Bush, firmó el viernes 23 en Miami la controvertida Acta para la Democracia en Cuba, conocida como ley Torricelli. Bush transformó la firma de la ley en unos de los últimos actos de su campaña electoral en Florida, en un intento por mantener a su lado a la comunidad de origen cubano.

La ley, contenida en una autorización de gastos de Defensa por valor de 247.000 millones de dólares, prohíbe a las empresas subsidarias estadounidenses en terceros países comerciar con el Gobierno de Fidel Castro. Los grandes ausentes en el acto fueron los principales promotores de la ley, los legisladores demócratas Robert Torricelli, representante por Nueva Jersey, y Bob Graham, senador por Florida, quienes no fueron invitados.

El presidente Bush se oponía inicialmente a la legislación anticipando el rechazo que produjo en países aliados como el Reino Unido, México, Canadá y Francia, que han protestado por la disposición, que consideran una intromisión de Washington en sus asuntos comerciales. Bush desoyó las peticiones de esos países de vetar la ley que ha firmado entre los entusiastas vivas de unos 600 ciudadanos americanos de origen cubano, que en su mayoría apoya al actual presidente. "Fidel Castro debe caer", dijo Bush a sus seguidores en Miami, y renovó su promesa de que seguirá luchando contra el régimen castrista "hasta que todas las familias cubanas estén unidas bajo la libertad."

TRANSLATION OF SPANISH NEWSPAPER TEXT

US toughens embargo against Cuba with the "Torricelli law"

Miami, US.10/28/92. The President of the United States, George Bush, signed, Friday the 23, in Miami, the controversial Act for Democracy in Cuba, known as the Torricelli law. Bush transformed the signing of the law into one of the last acts of his electoral campaign in Florida in an attempt to keep on his side the community of Cuban origin.

The law, contained in a Defense spending plan of 247, 000 million dollars, prohibits the subsidiaries of US companies in other countries from trading with the government of Fidel Castro. Noticeably absent form the signing were the two principles supporters of the law, the democratic legislators, Robert Torricelli, Representative from New Jersey, and Bob Graham, Senator from Florida, who were not invited.

President Bush initially opposed the legislation, anticipating the reaction it produced in allied countries such as the United Kingdom, Mexico, Canada and France, who have protested the bill, which they consider an intervention by Washington in their business affairs. Bush did not listen to the pleas to veto the law, which he instead signed in front of excited fans, some 600 American citizens of Cuban origin, who in their majority support the president. "Fidel Castro must fall," said Bush to his followers in Miami, and he renewed his promise that he will keep on fighting against Castro's regime "until all Cuban families are united in liberty."

TEXT B: L1 (ENGLISH) NEWSPAPER TEXT

Fujimori Seems to Win in Peru, a Voter Survey Says

LIMA, Peru. Nov 22. Surveys of voters leaving polling places today showed strong backing for President Alberto K. Fujimori's candidates for a Congress that will rewrite the Peruvian constitution. But it was unclear whether Mr. Fujimori had won the parlimentary majority he had sought.

The voting, seven months after Mr. Fujimori seized near-dictatorial powers by disbanding Congress and the courts and suspending the Constitution, consolidates his control over Government. He has said that he would interpret a victory today as a ringing endorsement of the measures he took on April 5.

Analysts said that despite the refusal by several large parties to take place in what they called illegal elections, a victory would give the administration a new measure of legitmacy with foreign governments, which have been highly critical of Mr. Fujimori's seizure of power.

Guerilla organizations had threatened to disrupt the elections for the Congress, which will have 80 members. But Peruvians turned out in large numbers, and guerilla violence was minor.

Around Lima, rebels set off several small bombs and threw sticks of dynamite near polling stations. Two people reportedly suffered minor injuries. No deaths were reported

The army and national police posted 100,000 troops around the country to guard polling stations. During the day, 250 observers from the Organization of American States were at voting centers around the country, trying to detect voting fraud and irregularities.

In Villa el Salvador, one of the largest shanty towns and a place where the Shining Path group of Maoist rebels has a strong presence, thousands of residents walked the sandy streets to a voting station in a run-down school. Many of those willing to express an opinion said they had supported Fujimori.

Official results are expected Monday.

TEXT C: L1 (ENGLISH) EXPOSITORY TEXT

Machines That Walk

Many machines imitate nature; a familiar example is the imitation of a soaring bird by the airplane. One form of animal locomotion that has resisted imitation is walking. Can it be that modern computers and feedback control systems make it possible to build machines that walk? We have been exploring the question with computer models and actual hardware.

One of the subjects of our attention is walking and running where balance plays a role. Until a century ago people still debated whether or not a horse in a trot had all of its legs off the ground simultaneously. The stop motion photography of Eadweard Muybridge settled the debate, showing that a horse does leave the ground entirely during a trot. A running person does so too, as does the dog, the cheetah and of course the kangaroo. Such animals not only walk, which requires dynamic balance, but also run, employing ballistic motions effectively to increase their rate of travel.

There are two fundamental difference between a crawling vehicle that is statically balanced and one that is dynamically balanced. The first difference is in the definition of stability. A crawling vehicle is stable if its legs provide at least a tripod of support at all times to ensure that it does not tip over; a dynamically balanced walking or running vehicle can be allowed to tip for brief intervals. Motions of the legs and the body ensure that a single tipping interval is brief and that an adequate base of support is maintained on the average. For example, a running man touches the ground alternately with his two legs, providing a base of support for his body only over time.

The second difference between static and dynamic balance is in the consideration of speed and momentum. Static balance assumes that the configuration of the supporting legs and the position of the center of gravity are adequate to specify stability; it ignores the vehicle's motion. Such static computations are not always sufficient. For example, a fast-moving vehicle might tip forward if it stopped suddenly with the center of gravity too close to the front legs. In order to understand the greater mobility of walking and running systems one must not relax the definition of stability and account for velocity in computing balance.

References

Ahmed, M. (1988). *Speaking as cognitive regulation: A study of L1 and L2 dyadic problem-solving activity.* Unpublished doctoral dissertation. University of Delaware.

Appel, G. (1986). *L1 and L2 narrative and expository discourse production: A Vygostkyan analysis.* Unpublished doctoral dissertation. University of Delaware.

Appel, G. & Lantolf, J. P. (1994). Speaking as mediation: A study of L1 and L2 text recall tasks. *The Modern Language Journal, 78,* 437-452.

Ballstaedt, S-P & Mandl, H. (1987). Influencing the degree of reading comprehension. In E. van der Meer & J. Hoffman (Eds.), *Knowledge aided information processing* (pp. 119-139). North Holland: Elsevier Science Publishing.

Bell, A. (1991). *The language of news media.* Oxford, UK: Blackwell.

Bernhardt, E. B. (1983). Testing foreign language reading comprehension: The immediate recall protocol. *Die Unterrichtspraxis, 16,* 17-33.

Bernhardt, E. B. (1987). Cognitive processes in L2: An examination of reading behaviors. In J. P. Lantolf & A. Labarca (Eds.), *Research in second language learning: Focus on the classroom* (pp. 35-50). Norwood, NJ: Ablex.

Bernhardt, E. B. (1990). A model of L2 text reconstruction: The recall of literary text by learners of German. In A. Labarca (Ed.), *Issues in L2: Theory as practice/practice as theory* (pp. 21-43). Norwood, NJ: Ablex.

Bernhardt, E. B (1991a). A psycholinguistic perspective on second language literacy. *AILA Review-Revue de AILA, 8,* 31-44.

Bernhardt, E. B. (1991b). *Reading development in a second language.* Norwood, NJ: Ablex.

Bernhardt, E. B. & Kamil, M. (1995). Interpreting relationships between L1 and L2 reading: Consolidating the linguistic threshold and the linguistic interdependence hypotheses. *Applied Linguistics, 16,* 15-34.

Blakar, R. & Rommetveit, R. (1975). Utterances 'in Vacuo' and in context. *Linguistics, 153,* 5-32.

Brooks, F. & Donato, R. (1994). Vygotskyan approaches to understanding foreign language learner discourse during communicative tasks. *Hispania, 77,* 262-274.

Bruner, J. (1973). *Beyond the information given: studies in the psychology of knowing.* New York: Norton

Carrell, P., Devine, J. & Eskey, D. (Eds.). (1988). *Interactive approaches to second language reading.* Cambridge: Cambridge University Press.

Carrell, P. (1983). Three components of background knowledge in reading comprehension. Language Learning, 33, 183-207.

Carrell, P. (1984a). The effects of rhetorical organization on ESL readers. *TESOL Quarterly, 18,* 441-469.

Carrell, P. (1984b). Evidence of a formal schema in second language comprehension. *Language Learning, 34,* 87-112.

Carrell, P. (1985). Facilitating ESL reading by teaching text structure. *TESOL Quarterly, 19,* 727-752.

Carrell, P. (1987). Content and formal schemata in ESL reading. *TESOL Quarterly, 21,* 461-481.

Channell, J. (1994). *Vague language.* Oxford: Oxford University Press.

Chomsky, N. (1972). *Language and mind.* San Diego: Harcout Brace Jovanovich.

Coughlin, P. & Duff, P. (1994). Same task, different activities: Analysis of a SLA task from an activity theory perspective. In J. P. Lantolf & G. Appel (Eds.), *Vygotskian approaches to second language research* (pp. 171-194). Norwood, NJ: Ablex.

Crookes, G. & Gass, S. (Eds.). (1993a). *Tasks and language learning: Integrating theory and practice.* Clevedon, UK: Multilingual Matters.

Crookes, G. & Gass, S. (Eds.). (1993b). *Tasks in a pedagogical context: Integrating theory and practice.* Clevedon, UK: Multilingual Matters.

Davis, J. N., Lange, D. L. & Samuels, S. J. (1988). Effects of text structure instruction on foreign language readers' recall of a scientific journal article. *Journal of Reading Behavior, 20,* 203-214.

DiCamilla, F. (1991). *Private speech and private writing: A study of given/new information and modality in student compositions.* Unpublished doctoral dissertation. University of Delaware

DiCamilla, F. & Lantolf, J. P. (1994). The linguistics analysis of private writing. *Language Sciences, 16,* 347-369

van Dijk, T. & Kintsch, W. (1983). *Strategies of discourse comprehension.* Orlando, FL: Academic Press.

Donato, R. & Lantolf, J. P. (1990) The dialogic origins of L2 monitoring. Pragmatics and *Language Learning, 1,* 83-98.

Flavell, J. H. (1966). Le langue privé. *Bulletin de Psychologie, 19,* 698-701.

Floyd, P. & Carrell, P. (1987). Effects on ESL reading of cultural content schemata. *Language Learning, 37,* 89-108.

Frawley, W. (1987). *Text and epistemology.* Norwood, NJ. Ablex

Frawley, W. (1992). *The cross cultural study of private speech.* Paper presented at the First Conference for Socio-cultural Research, Symposium of Private Speech and Self-regulation, Madrid.

Frawley, W. & Lantolf, J. P (1984). Speaking and self-order: A critique of orthodox L2 research. *Studies in Second Language Education, 6,* 143-159.

Frawley, W. & Lantolf, J. P. (1985). Second language discourse: A Vygotskyan perspective. *Applied Linguistics, 6,* 19-44.

Givón, T. (1982). Evidentiality an epistemic space. *Studies in Language, 6,* 23-49.

Grabe, W. (1991). Current developments in second language reading research. *TESOL Quarterly, 25,* 375-406.

Grice, H. P. (1975). Logic and conversation. In P. Cole & J. Morgan (Eds.), *Speech acts vol. 3: Syntax and Semantics* (pp. 41-58). New York: Academic Press.

Harré, R. & Gillett, G. (1994). *The discursive mind.* Thousand Oaks, CA: Sage.

Horiba, Y. (1993). The role of causal reasoning and language competence in narrative comprehension. *Studies in Second Language Acquisition, 15,* 459-472.

Horiba, Y., van den Broek, P. W., & Fletcher, C. R. (1993). Second language readers' memory for narrative texts: Evidence for structure-preserving top-down processing. *Language Learning, 43,* 345-372.

John-Steiner, V. (1985a). *Notebooks of the mind. Explorations of thinking.* New York: Harper and Row.

John-Steiner, V. (1985b). The road to competency in an alien land. In J. V. Werstch (Ed.), *Culture, communication, and cognition: Vygotskian perspectives* (pp. 348-372). Cambridge: Cambridge University Press.

John-Steiner, V. (1992). Private speech among adults. In R. M. Diaz and L. E. Berk (Eds.), *Private Speech: From social interaction to self-regulation* (pp. 285-296). Hillsdale, NJ: Lawrence Erlbaum.

Johnson, P. (1981). The effects on reading comprehension of building background knowledge. *TESOL Quarterly, 16,* 503-516.

Johnston, P. H. (1983). *Reading comprehension assessment: A cognitive basis.* Newark, DE: International Reading Association.

Kintsch, W. (1977). On comprehending stories. In M. Just & P. A. Carpenter (Eds.), *Cognitive processes in comprehension* (pp. 33-62). Hillsdale, NJ: Lawrence Erlbaum Associates.

Kintsch, W. (1993). Information accretion and reduction in text processing: Inferences. *Discourse Processes, 16,* 193-202.

Kintsch, W. & E. Greene. (1978). The role of culture-specific schemata in the comprehension and recall of stories. *Discourse Processes, 1,* 1-13.

Kozulin, A. (1986). The concept of activity in Soviet Psychology. *American Psychologist, 41,* 264-274.

Kozulin, A. (1990). *Vygotsky's psychology: A biography of ideas.* Cambridge, MA: Harvard University Press.

Kramsch, C. & Nolden, T. (1994) Redefining literacy in a foreign language. *Die Unterrichtspraxis, 27,* 28-35.

Lakoff, G. & Johnson, M. (1980). *Metaphors we live by.* Chicago: University of Chicago Press.

Lantolf, J. P. , DiCamilla, F. & Ahmed, M. (1996) The cognitive function of linguistic performance: tense/aspect use by L1 and L2 speakers. *Language Sciences, 19,* 153-165.

Lantolf, J. P. & Appel, G. (1994). Theoretical framework: An introduction to Vygotskian perspectives on second language research. In J. P. Lantolf and G. Appel, (Eds.), *Vygotskian approaches to second language research* (pp. 1-32). Norwood, NJ: Ablex.

Lee, J. F. (1986). On the use of the recall task to measure L2 reading comprehension. *Studies in Second Language Acquisition, 8,* 201-212.

Lee, J. F. (1990). Constructive processes evidenced by early stage non-native readers of Spanish in comprehending an expository text. *Hispanic Linguistics, 4,* 129-148.

Lee, J. F. & Riley, G. L. (1990). The effect of prereading rhetorically-oriented frameworks on the recall of two structurally different expository texts. *Studies in Second Language Acquisition, 12,* 25-41.

Leontiev, A. A. (1981). *Psychology and the language learning process.* Oxford: Pergamon Press.

Leontiev, A. N. (1981). The problem of activity in psychology. In J.V. Wertsch (Ed.), *The concept of activity in Soviet psychology* (pp. 37-71). Armonk, NY: ME Sharpe, Inc.

Luria, A. (1973). *The working brain: An introduction to neuropsychology.* (B. Haigh, Trans.). New York: Basic Books.

Mandler, J. M. & Johnson, N. S. (1977). Remembrance of things parsed: Story structure and recall. *Cognitive Psychology, 9,* 111-151.

Markovà, I. (1992). On structure and dialogicity in Prague semiotics. In A. H. Wold (Ed.), *The dialogical alternative: Towards a theory of language and mind,* (pp. 45-63). Oslo: Scandinavian University Press.

McCafferty, S. (1992). The use of private speech by adult second language learners: A cross cultural study. *The Modern Language Journal, 76,* 179-189.

McCafferty, S. (1994a). The use of private speech by adults ESL learners at different levels of proficiency. In J. P. Lantolf & G. Appel, (Eds.), *Vygotskian approaches to second language research* (pp. 171-194). Norwood, NJ: Ablex.

McCafferty, S. (1994b). Adult second language learners' use of private speech: A review of studies. *The Modern Language Journal, 78,* 421-436.

McCafferty, S. (1996). The use of non-verbal forms of expression in relation to L2 private speech. *Cornell Working Papers in Linguistics, 14,* 101-124.

McCafferty, S. (1998). Non-verbal expression and L2 private speech. *Applied Linguistics, 19,* 73-96.

McNeil, D. (1992). *Hand and mind: What gestures reveal about thought.* Chicago: University of Chicago Press.

Mehler, J. & Noizet, G. (1973). *Textes pour une psycholinguistique.* Paris: Mouton.

Miller, G. A. & Johnson-Laird, P. N. (Eds.). (1976). *Language and perception.* Cambridge: Cambridge University Press.

Nunan, D. (1989). *Designing tasks for the communicative classroom.* Cambridge: Cambridge University Press.

Osgood, C. & Sebeok, T. (1965). *Psycholinguistics: A survey of research and theory problems.* Bloomington, IN: University of Indiana Press.

Reddy, M. (1979). The conduit metaphor—a case of conflict in our language about language. In A. Ortony (Ed.), *Metaphor and thought* (pp. 284-324). Cambridge: Cambridge University Press.

Roller, C. M & Matambo, A. R. (1992) Bilingual readers' use of background knowledge in learning from text. *TESOL Quarterly, 26,* 129-141.

Rommetveit, R. (1991). Psycholinguistics, hermaneutics, and cognitive science. In G. Appel & H. W. Dechert (Eds.), *The case for psycholinguistic cases* (pp. 1-15). Amsterdam/Philadelphia: John Benjamins.

Rommetveit, R. (1992). Outlines of a dialogically based social-cognitive approach to human cognition and communication. In A. H. Wold (Ed.), *The dialogical alternative: Towards a theory of language and mind* (pp. 19-44). Oslo: Scandinavian University Press.

Rumelhart, D. E. (1980). Schemata: The building blocks of cognition. In R. Spiro, B. Bruce & W. Brewer (Eds.), *Theoretical issues in reading comprehension* (pp. 33-58). Hillsdale, NJ: Lawrence Erlbaum.

Samuels, S. J. & Kamil, M. L. (1984). Models of the reading process. In P. Carrell, J. Devine & D. Eskey (Eds.), *Interactive approaches to second language reading* (pp. 22-36) Cambridge: Cambridge University Press.

Scribner, S & Cole, M. (1973). Cognitive consequences of formal and informal education. *Science, 182*, 553-559.

Scribner, S. & Cole, M. (1981). *The psychology of literacy.* Cambridge, MA: Harvard University Press.

Smirnov, A. A. (1973). Problems of the psychology of memory. New York: Plenum.

Soskin, W. F & John, V. (1963). The study of spontaneous talk. In G. Barker (Ed.), *The stream of behavior: Explorations of its structure and content* (pp. 228-281). New York: MIT Press.

Steffenson, M. S. & Joag-Dev, M. L. (1984). Cultural knowledge and reading. In J. C. Alderson & A. H. Urquhart (Eds.), *Reading in a foreign language* (pp. 48-64). London: Longman.

Swaffar, J. (1988). Readers, texts and second languages: The interactive processes. *Modern Language Journal, 72*, 123-149.

Swaffar, J., Arens, K. & Byner, H. (1991). *Reading for meaning.* Englewood Cliffs, NJ: Prentice Hall.

Talyzina, N. (1981). *The psychology of learning: theories of learning and programmed instruction.* Moscow: Progress Press.

Tchudi, S. (1986). *Teaching writing in the content areas: College level.* Washington, DC. National Educational Association.

Trabasso, T. & Suh, S. (1993). Understanding text: Achieving explanatory coherence through on-line inferences and mental operations in working memory. *Discourse Processes, 16*, 3-34.

Trabasso, T & Magliano, J. (1996). Conscious understanding during comprehension. *Discourse Processes, 21*, 255-287.

Urquhart, A. H. (1984). The effect of rhetorical ordering on readability. In J. C. Alderson & A. H. Urquhart (Eds.), *Reading in a foreign language* (pp. 160-175). London: Longman.

Vygotsky, L. S. (1978). *Mind in society: The development of higher mental functions.* Cambridge, MA: Harvard University Press.

Vygotsky, L. S. (1986). *Thought and language* (A. Kozulin, Trans.). Cambridge, MA: MIT Press.

Wertsch, J. V. (1979). The regulation of human interaction and the given-new organization of private speech. In G. Ziven (Ed.), *The development of Self-regulation through private speech* (pp. 79-98). New York: Wiley.

Wertsch, J. V. (Ed.). (1981a). *The concept of activity in Soviet psychology.* Armonk, NY: M.E. Sharpe, Inc.

Wertsch, J. V. (1981b). The concept of activity in Soviet psychology: An introduction. In J. V. Wertsch, (Ed.), *The concept of activity in Soviet psychology* (pp. 3-36). Armonk, NY: ME Sharpe, Inc.

Wertsch, J. V. (Ed.). (1985a). *Culture, communication, and cognition: Vygotskian perspectives.* Cambridge: Cambridge University Press.

Wertsch, J. V. (1985b). *Vygotsky and the social formation of mind.* Cambridge, MA: Harvard University Press.

Wertsch, J. V. (1991). *Voices of the mind: A sociocultural approach to mediated action.* Cambridge, MA: Harvard University Press.

Wittgenstein, L. (1953). *Philosophical investigations.* (G. E. Anscombre, Trans.). Oxford: Blackwell.

Wold, A. H. (1992) Introduction. In A .H. Wold (Ed), *The dialogical alternative: Towards a theory of language and mind* (pp. 1-18). Oslo: Scandinavian University Press.

Zwaan, R. & Brown, C. (1996). The influence of language proficiency and comprehension skill on situation-model construction. *Discourse Processes, 21,* 289-327.

Author Index

Subject Index

A

abbreviation 26, 27, 53, 62, 67, 70, 73, 84, 85, 95, 104-105, 107

abstract component 44-46, 66, 67

action 17- 21, 23, 25, 108, 126
  distinction between action and operation 19
  execution 20, 21, 24, 25
  goal 14, 18-24, 38, 70, 93, 95, 97, 102, 106-108, 121, 125-128
  goal-directedness 18-22
  orienting component 20, 21
  subgoals 19, 21, 70, 102, 108-110, 111

activity 12-28, 32, 36-38, 42, 61, 65-71, 91-98, 102-116, 120-128
  and the study of consciousness 12-14
  features of 17, 23
  levels of 17 - 20
  self-directed 66, 67
  versus task 21-24, 60, 125, 126

activity potentials 23-24

Activity Theory 13, 15, 17, 18-21, 24, 38
  appropriation 17, 25, 68, 69
  condition 18-21, 23
  genetic explanation 17, 33, 38
  motive 14, 17-22, 37
  operation 17-21

social interaction 17, 37

ad hoc categories 53, 82

attention 54, 57, 68, 82, 97, 119

behavior 11, 14, 124
  mental 14, 16, 25, 32, 38, 124
  physical 12, 14, 16, 25, 38, 124

B

Behaviorism and reflexology 11, 13, 15, 16, 32,

C

cognitive distance 31, 32, 43, 82, 92, 111, 116, 121

cognitive processes 12, 128
  (see also mental functions)

cognitive science 11, 14

cohesion 70, 74, 75, 90, 91, 92, 100, 105-107, 109, 111, 112, 128

communicative activity 2, 44

concept formation 14

conduit metaphor 2, 4, 5, 8-10

consciousness 11-16, 24, 37, 38, 57, 124
  definition 12-15
  and discourse 15, 17
  and language 11-16, 24, 33, 57
  as object of study 11, 12, 16
  observation of 12, 14, 16, 20, 24
  organization 13-14, 16-17, 124